9/22

Rahul

Rahul

JATIN GANDHI AND VEENU SANDHU

PENGUIN
VIKING

VIKING
Published by the Penguin Group
Penguin Books India Pvt. Ltd, 11 Community Centre, Panchsheel Park,
New Delhi 110 017, India
Penguin Group (USA) Inc., 375 Hudson Street, New York, New York 10014,
USA
Penguin Group (Canada), 90 Eglinton Avenue East, Suite 700, Toronto,
Ontario, M4P 2Y3, Canada (a division of Pearson Penguin Canada Inc.)
Penguin Books Ltd, 80 Strand, London WC2R 0RL, England
Penguin Ireland, 25 St Stephen's Green, Dublin 2, Ireland (a division of
Penguin Books Ltd)
Penguin Group (Australia), 250 Camberwell Road, Camberwell, Victoria
3124, Australia (a division of Pearson Australia Group Pty Ltd)
Penguin Group (NZ), 67 Apollo Drive, Rosedale, Auckland 0632,
New Zealand (a division of Pearson New Zealand Ltd)
Penguin Group (South Africa) (Pty) Ltd, 24 Sturdee Avenue, Rosebank,
Johannesburg 2196, South Africa

Penguin Books Ltd, Registered Offices: 80 Strand, London WC2R 0RL, England

First published in Viking by Penguin Books India 2012

Copyright © Jatin Gandhi and Veenu Sandhu 2012

10 9 8 7 6 5 4 3 2 1

The views and opinions expressed in this book are the authors' own and the
facts are as reported by them which have been verified to the extent possible,
and the publishers are not in any way liable for the same.

ISBN 9780670084807

Typeset in Dante MT by Eleven Arts, New Delhi
Printed at Manipal Technologies Ltd, Manipal

Contents

Preface   vii

Introduction   1

The Inevitable: Death and Politics   33

Sonia to Rahul via Priyanka   52

The Shaping of the Personality   80

Between Two Plenaries: The Rise of Rahul Gandhi   102

12 Tughlaq Lane   120

Youth Express   138

Building Brand Rahul   159

The Dalit Agenda   184

Mission 2012 Recast   200

Epilogue   222

Select Bibliography   258

Preface

'Isn't it too early to write a biography of Rahul Gandhi?' was a question that we were often asked when we set out on this project about one and a half years ago. It was also one of the first questions we asked Penguin India when we were approached with the proposal. As we became convinced a book on the subject was in order, the map for it evolved.

We saw that Rahul Gandhi had ideas about revolutionizing youth politics that he was slowly putting into place. One look at the websites of the Indian Youth Congress (IYC) and the National Students' Union of India (NSUI) now and you know the plan to revive these frontal organizations is nothing short of a mammoth management project targeting a few crore young people. This was something unprecedented in the history of India's youth politics. As the year 2011 drew to a close, the IYC had an active membership base of one crore—a big number even for a country with a population more than a hundred times that number. Consider this: In the 2009 Lok Sabha elections, at less than 60 per cent polling, under 42 crore votes were polled. Combine the targeted membership of the NSUI and the IYC, and the number of dedicated workers—two crore—suddenly becomes an important statistic not just in youth politics but also in electoral politics. With this army of young workers at different levels, the Congress could hold considerable sway over a large number of voters. The revolution in youth politics could usher in far-reaching changes in the politics of the country and ultimately impact all our lives. Yet, for that to happen, a mere plan is not enough. The plan would have to work, and for that to happen, several hurdles would have to be overcome.

This book is not exactly a SWOT analysis of Rahul Gandhi's plans and the Congress's prospects, but it does aspire, through the course of its narrative, to tell the story of what he is up to and how it will affect not just the voter but the average Indian. As the book goes to print, Rahul's mark on day-to-day politics can be seen everywhere, whether it is the 2012 assembly elections in Uttar Pradesh, the country's struggle against corruption, or special relief packages for weavers running into a few thousand crore rupees. He is influencing which side the government must take in the tug of war over land and minerals between corporate giants and tribals. Rahul got the Congress to widen its traditional focus on the *garib* (poor) to include the *aam aadmi* (common man). We know, for instance, from D.K. Singh's April 2010 report in the *Indian Express*, that from 2007 to 2009, Rahul wrote nine letters to the prime minister on varied subjects, including his concerns about public health, climate change and water. Another report, by Diptosh Majumdar in the *Times of India*, in October 2011, revealed that Rahul wrote seventeen letters to the prime minister in the United Progressive Alliance's second stint, increasing both the frequency and the scope of his interventions. In one such letter, he suggested that it was not enough for ministers to declare merely their own net worth, they should also declare those of their families.

In the age of coalition politics, where allies can make or break a party, Rahul has caused a shake-up within the Congress by questioning certain old and tested alliances. The last single-party government with a clear majority was led by Rajiv Gandhi. For over twenty years, successive governments have counted on external support, including the backing of small regional parties, to stay in power. And now a man still considered a political novice by many is working on the conviction that the Congress Party ought to do without burdensome allies. Rahul wants the Party to regain the dominance it enjoyed many decades ago.

The Indian National Congress's dominance over the country's politics was both inspired and consolidated by the nationalist movement that it led. A vast majority rallied around the Party during the nationalist movement and the trend continued well beyond Independence, till the 1967 general elections. If the nationalist spirit was the magnet that brought large numbers into the Congress fold and kept them there, Rahul hopes the aspirations of the country's youth will now act as the binding agent. The average age of the Indian today is around twenty-six years, and two-thirds of the country's population is under thirty-five. There are multiple and long-term advantages for a political formation targeting the young. Under Rahul, the IYC and the NSUI have set out to do precisely that for the Congress: draw young men and women into the Party's fold. Despite its jibes, the principal opposition party, the Bharatiya Janata Party, does not have a counterpart to Rahul, who is, at forty-one, a young man in present-day politics.

We are at an interesting phase in Indian—and Congress—politics. It's a time when the ageing old guard is slowly and, at times, reluctantly making way for the younger lot represented, at least within the Congress, by Rahul. The army of young people he is building includes those who have never really given politics a serious thought or have family members even remotely associated with politics. There are some who have simply given up well-paying jobs, even outside the country, to join him. It's a phenomenon that hasn't been witnessed in Indian politics in a long time, perhaps since the days before Independence.

That Rahul Gandhi belongs to a political dynasty and yet aspires to create a Congress where merit is not devoured by dynastic succession is a contradiction that throws up a whole range of interesting possibilities and challenges. We have tried to look at these challenges through the prism of unfolding political events. The party to which Rahul belongs is the frontrunner when it comes to promoting and exalting dynasty. How then will the newest dynast succeed in challenging this issue within the Congress? It was essential to touch upon the history of the Nehru–Gandhi family to understand what has brought Rahul to the juncture at which he stands today, and how it affects his politics. This book, therefore, is also a brief story of the events that shaped the man as much as it is about the events he is shaping. We have gone back, again briefly, into his childhood and his growing-up years to get a sense of the events—the tragedies, and the political and personal fallouts of those tragedies—that kept him from having a 'regular' life and ended up shaping his personality.

The people who are part of Rahul Gandhi's inner circle and his army of foot soldiers form an important aspect of this book. They help us gauge his intentions. We have spoken to people situated at various levels in his team. Our request to interview Rahul was turned down. Kanishka Singh, a core member of Rahul's team and a close confidant, called back to say that Rahul felt that it was too early for a book on him and that an interview would seem like an endorsement of the book. We left it at that. The only endorsement we seek is from our readers. Every other journalist who has tried to learn directly from Rahul his views on crucial matters has run into the same problem of access. In June 2010, a columnist with the *Wall Street Journal* wrote: 'The Gandhis are probably the most opaque major politicians in the democratic world. They rarely speak to the media, and when they do, it's not to critics.'

Being journalists, we were able to speak with a fairly large number of politicians and members of Parliament, across parties, during the course of our work. There were some among them who took time out to grant us separate interviews for the book. We are grateful to one and all—those who spoke to us on the record and those who shared information on the condition that their names be withheld. Some of the young foot soldiers in the IYC and the NSUI were more forthcoming, and we are grateful to them for giving us crucial insights into the grassroots movement that started with Rahul's advent in politics.

Uttar Pradesh and the Congress's Dalit politics in the state are other crucial aspects of this book. Rahul has been working with the conviction that the only thing that can ensure the return of the Congress to its past strength is its revival in India's Hindi belt. The Bihar assembly results were a big setback to the Party in 2010 and there is a lot at stake for Rahul and the Congress in Uttar Pradesh in 2012. Right from the beginning, Uttar Pradesh has been his focus and Mayawati among his prime targets.

In the years that he has been in politics, Rahul seems to have, by and large, based his politics on a few major issues: the problems of the poor and the marginalized, whether it is the farmers, the tribals or the Dalits. Hence we also take a close look at the careful branding exercise in which the Congress and the people around him work overtime to depict him as the messiah of the marginalized and the voice of the underdog, as well as his own efforts in connecting with the poor.

∗∗∗

More than just a special word of gratitude is due to Hartosh Singh Bal, fellow journalist and long-time friend, for his incisive interventions and suggestions at different stages of the book. We also thank our editors at Penguin, Ranjana Sengupta for her help from the very beginning and R. Sivapriya for bringing this chapter successfully to a close, and Paloma Dutta, our copy editor for this book.

A bunch of other friends in the media helped us during the course of writing this book. We thank Rasheed Kidwai, Sanjeev Ratna Singh, Pallavi Ghosh, Ravi Dhiman, Subodh Ghildiyal, Nandita Suneja Baruah, Sandeep Phukan, Dhirendra K. Jha, Madhavdas Gopalakrishnan, Aresh Shirali and D.K. Singh who exchanged notes and ideas with us or whose reports were a great help to this project. This book would not have even taken off without the generous permission and encouragement of our respective editors at *Open*, NDTV and *Business Standard*.

We are grateful to the Nehru Memorial Museum and Library for allowing access to their collection of books as well as the Lok Sabha secretariat for the various documents, archives and access to Parliament; and the team at pressbrief.in for the treasure trove of information and recordings on the Gandhi family. Tonusree Basu and M.R. Madhavan at PRS Legislative Research provided useful insights and statistics for the project and deserve a special mention here. So does Rajkumar Srivastava at the Indian Express Archive who offered important suggestions and some wonderful options when we were selecting the pictures.

Uday Shankar, who was the news director at Star News in 2005, deserves a 'thank you' for saying at that point in time: 'Rahul Gandhi is not just a person, he is a full-fledged beat. Cover him like that.'

7 December 2011
New Delhi

Introduction

Rain clouds were beginning to gather over Amethi. A young man in a white kurta–pyjama sat on the lawn under a darkening sky, speaking to journalists about a commitment he had recently made. It was the April of 2004. Less than a month earlier, on 21 March, the Congress had announced that Rahul Gandhi, the fifth-generation heir of the Nehru–Gandhi dynasty, would contest for the Lok Sabha from Amethi in Uttar Pradesh.

'I could have joined politics soon after my father died,' Rahul told his interviewer, Vrinda Gopinath of the *Indian Express*. But he hadn't because he felt he was very young and 'had nothing to offer'. The conviction of the man who had just taken his first step into politics that he could have stepped into his father's shoes with ease thirteen years earlier, is a telling comment on the complexion of the party to which he belongs—the Indian National Congress—and that of Indian politics which has found it practically impossible to wean itself away from dynasties.

The last thirty years or so, since the death of Sanjay Gandhi, have shown what the Congress intrinsically believes—that a Gandhi can be replaced only by a Gandhi. For almost a century now, a Nehru–Gandhi has always held a key position within the Congress, and in those brief periods when the family has chosen to remain outside active politics, it has run the show from behind the scenes. The Nehru–Gandhi clan, one of the world's oldest political dynasties, will have it no other way. The Congress, too, is most comfortable when someone from the family is in charge.

Motilal Nehru, the lawyer-politician to whom the Nehru–Gandhi dynasty owes its origin, was Congress president twice, in 1919 and then in 1928. His son Jawaharlal's tryst with politics started in 1916 at the age of twenty-seven and, thirteen years later, in 1929, he took over from Motilal as Congress president. On the face of it, the succession happened through a democratic process, and Jawaharlal was made Congress president only after an election. But, being the son of an illustrious leader and having the backing of the country's most towering personality, Mohandas Karamchand Gandhi, he had an undeniable advantage over the others. That he was well-educated and gave a voice to the emotions and ideas of the youth in a manner no one before him had done further tilted the scales in his favour. M.J. Akbar, in his book *Nehru: The Making of India*, describes that historic moment in time when Jawaharlal was elected party president, though not without resentment in some quarters. On 13 July 1929, Motilal wrote to Gandhi making a case for his son, Jawaharlal. Gandhi, he wrote, must accept that:

> The revolt of the youth has become an accomplished fact . . . It would be sheer flattery to say that you [Gandhi] have today the same influence as you had over the youth of the country some years ago, and most of them make no secret of the fact. All this would indicate that the need of the hour is the lead of Gandhi and the voice of Jawahar . . . There are strong reasons for either you or Jawahar to wear the crown, and if you and Jawahar stand together, as to which there is no doubt in my mind, it does not really matter who it is that stands in front and who behind.

By this time, an anti-Nehru lobby had already grown within the Congress. It tried to derail Motilal's plans by putting up its own candidate, Sardar Vallabhbhai Patel. And though Patel enjoyed greater support than Jawaharlal among the provincial Congress committees, everybody knew in their hearts that Gandhi would have the final say in the matter. To his credit, Jawaharlal himself was far from keen on wearing the 'crown'. On 9 July 1929, he wrote to Gandhi: 'I am very nervous about the matter and do not like the idea at all.' In August, despite Jawaharlal's reservations, Gandhi publicly suggested that Motilal's son be made Congress president. When he learnt of this, Jawaharlal, who was in Calcutta, sent a telegram to Gandhi begging him not to insist on his name for presidentship. But Gandhi had made up his mind and, on 28 September 1929, he told the All India Congress Committee (AICC) to elect Jawaharlal. What was meant to be an election was, in fact, the Congress bowing to Gandhi's diktat. Despite visible resentment from some quarters, on paper, everybody voted for Jawaharlal.

Describing the third generation witnessing the transition of power from the first generation to the second, Jad Adams and Phillip Whitehead, in their book *The Dynasty: The Nehru-Gandhi Story*, write:

Gandhi had put Jawaharlal's name forward for the presidency of the 1929 Congress at Lahore, a vitally important occasion. Jawaharlal was somewhat embarrassed and tried to refuse the honour, but Motilal was overjoyed, quoting the Persian adage, 'What the father is unable to accomplish, the son achieves.' Indira, now aged twelve, was present to see the transfer of power from father to son.

Thirty-five years later, the Indian National Congress would witness another attempt at a dynastic succession, this time from father to daughter. Barely three days after Jawaharlal's death in 1964, Congress leader Lal Bahadur Shastri approached Indira and said, *'Ab aap mulk ko sambhal leejiye* (Now you take over the responsibility of the country).' The belief ingrained in Indian culture that the right of first refusal lies with the son or the daughter in a succession plan permeates Indian politics as well. Katherine Frank writes in *Indira: The Life of Indira Nehru Gandhi* that other Congress leaders also approached Indira mainly because, being Jawaharlal's daughter, the issue of her candidacy had to be clarified first. The invitation to Indira to assume prime ministership was apparently made out of courtesy rather than a serious desire to see her at the helm of the country's affairs. The actual succession battle was between Lal Bahadur Shastri and Morarji Desai. But, had the grieving Indira taken up the offer, Congress leaders might have had to accept her decision. Backed by Congress president K. Kamaraj and the syndicate, Shastri was eventually the Party's unanimous choice. On the evening of 1 June 1964, the day the decision was taken, he called on Indira again after visiting Jawaharlal's cremation site. Once again, he suggested to her that she become prime minister even though the fact was that, at this stage, he was in no position to make such an offer to her. The next day, when he rose to speak in Parliament after acting prime minister Gulzarilal Nanda proposed his name as party leader, Shastri first lauded Indira and said he looked forward to her 'continued association with us'. He went to the extent of saying that it was imperative to 'have a Nehru in the Cabinet to maintain stability', and promptly offered her the position of minister of information and broadcasting.

One and a half years later, when Shastri died, Kamaraj and other Congress leaders decided to make the forty-eight-year-old Indira his successor. Kamaraj succeeded in persuading all the other candidates, except Morarji Desai, to withdraw. During the vote in Parliament, the scales were tilted decisively in Indira's favour. She received 355 votes against Desai's 169. Zareer Masani, in his book

Indira Gandhi: A Biography, talks about how an otherwise-harsh critic of Indira's, her paternal aunt Vijaya Lakshmi Pandit, former governor of Maharashtra and member of Parliament (MP) from Phulpur in Uttar Pradesh, issued a statement: 'We Nehrus are very proud of our family. When a Nehru is chosen as prime minister, the people will rejoice.' On 24 January 1966, Indira was sworn in as prime minister of India. The dynasty had established strong roots within the Party; Indira would only nurture it further.

Some records indicate that Nehru was not in favour of Indira being promoted by the Party. On 2 February 1959, when she was formally elected president of the Indian National Congress, Jawaharlal had disapproved of the move. Not only was he doubtful of Indira's political abilities, he was also worried about the impression her elevation would give, writes his sister Krishna Nehru Hutheesing in her book *Dear to Behold: An Intimate Portrait of Indira Gandhi*. Jawaharlal had said that he 'would not like to appear to encourage some dynastic arrangement. That would be wholly undemocratic and an undesirable thing.' However, journalist Kuldip Nayar writes in his book *India: The Critical Years*, published in 1971, that many senior Congress leaders of that time—including Kamaraj, S. Nijalingappa and even

Shastri—thought Jawaharlal had Indira in his mind as his successor.

When Shastri was home minister I had occasion to talk to him on various matters. Once I ventured to ask him: 'Who do you think Nehru has in mind as his successor?' 'His daughter,' Shastri said without even a second's pause, as if he had already pondered over the problem. 'But it will not be easy,' he added. Referring to this observation, which appeared in my book *Between the Lines*, Mrs Gandhi has said: 'Had this been in my father's mind, surely he would have wanted me to be elected in Parliament. However, whenever the suggestion was made he agreed that I should not go into Parliament.' I don't want to join issue with her but Shastri did tell me that Nehru did have his daughter in mind as his successor. We were talking in Hindi and Shastri said, '*Unke dil mein siraf unki ladki hai* (He only has his daughter in mind).'

For the Congress, too, every time it has found itself in need of a successor, a Nehru–Gandhi has been the most desirable and, in fact, the only choice. Rahul, by entering politics, was only following a pattern set by his predecessors and the Party to which he belongs. And herein lies the contradiction: a dynasty flourishing within a democracy. In India, such contradictions have always coexisted and go beyond politics. Their roots lie in the socio-cultural fabric of the Indian subcontinent where the family name takes precedence over almost everything else. Every village, town and city has a few prominent families which are considered the repositories of power in that area. Their wealth and influence compensate for any lack of individual achievement, and the status that members of the family enjoy is often inherited but not necessarily earned. It is not a mere coincidence that in business, too, the family name—Tata, Birla, Ambani, Munjal, Godrej, Jindal, Oberoi—determines how powerful and financially strong the company is perceived to be.

In public perception, family name and family values matter. The Gandhis realize this and have made sure that they possess both in abundance. Dynasties, like that of the Nehru–Gandhis, are the crème de la crème of the Indian urban élite. Yet, to remain acceptable to the masses, they have to balance contemporaneity with tradition. Sonia's complete Indianization (she is always seen in a sari or a salwar–kameez); Rahul's white kurta–pyjama when he's campaigning, visiting villages or attending Parliament; and Priyanka's clothes (always a sari) when she is in Amethi or Rae Bareli, are calibrated decisions aimed at making the right impression and living up to the image of being a truly Indian family.

That Sonia was the ideal bahu in contrast to Maneka, Sanjay Gandhi's wife, has been widely discussed. Frank uses adjectives like 'garrulous', 'loud', 'boisterous' and 'uninhibited' to describe Maneka. In stark contrast to her sister-in-law, Maneka 'could not and would not adapt to the Gandhi household' and 'could also be disrespectful of her mother-in-law', something that was unthinkable for Sonia. Maneka later confessed that she 'didn't know housework and didn't want to learn cooking'. Sonia was at the other end of the spectrum and is often eulogized as the ideal wife, the ideal daughter-in-law and the ideal mother. Though we have very little access to her private life, her understanding of Indian handicrafts and her cooking abilities are well known. These are precisely the qualities which the ordinary Indian expects in a woman. The Gandhis have to be seen as entirely submitting and ascribing to the values of an Indian family. The relationship between the Gandhi family and Indian culture is a symbiotic one, a two-way process.

Another reason why dynasties continue to be accepted in the Indian context is the tradition of royalty. At the time of Independence, the country was a cluster of small kingdoms and principalities. The ruling classes of India whether in business or politics—which often interpenetrate each other, with businessmen exercising considerable political clout and successful politicians possessing vast business interests—often aspire to and follow in the footsteps of kings and princes in behaviour and lifestyle. It sets the members of the ruling class apart from the masses, making them attractive to the *aam aadmi*. Though, over the last fifty years or so, a slow revision has happened, thousands of small towns and villages of India are yet to break out of this mindset.

Political dynasties, however, are not the same as royal dynasties which demand unquestioning acceptance from the people. While there is no denying that political dynasties stand in conflict with the principles of democracy, it is equally important to acknowledge that they do not, and cannot, negate the foundation on which a democracy is built. The dynast does get the initial advantage which comes with the family name and the goodwill which the earlier generation of leaders from the family may have acquired. But, once voted into power, he has to prove himself worthy of people's trust even if he is allowed more concessions than a first-generation politician would be granted. Yet, for the dynast to be rejected by the people, he would have to do a great deal of wrong in public perception. While there are examples of the voter turning his back on powerful and charismatic dynasts, India's political history also shows that the Indian electorate is more forgiving of their mistakes. Indira's example is a case in point.

The politician who displayed shades of dictatorship by imposing Emergency when she felt that her position in the government was being threatened was ousted from office in the next election. Even then, it took the excesses of Emergency and a powerful political movement led by Jai Prakash Narayan (JP) to overthrow her. More than fifty Congress leaders defected to JP's side and an even greater number wanted Indira replaced. The day she lost, India celebrated the way it had on the eve of Independence. But, less than three years later, in 1980, the same electorate which had rejoiced over her defeat with fireworks and drumbeats voted her back to power with a thumping majority. The Congress won 353 of the 529 seats.

Rahul's father, Rajiv, is another example of how Indian voters are quite capable of pulling the carpet from under any politician's feet, exercising the power which ultimately rests with them: the power of the ballot. If Rajiv was elected with a sweeping majority because the people's sympathies lay with him after the brutal assassination of his mother, he was also shunted out fast when the same people felt betrayed by the dynast whose

'Mr Clean' image had taken a beating after a series of scandals in the government.

On more than one occasion, Rahul has said that he cannot deny the fact that he is a dynast and that his great-grandfather, his grandmother and his father were all prime ministers of India. Speaking to students at Jim Corbett National Park in Uttarakhand in 2008, he said:

> If I had not come from my family, I wouldn't be here. You can enter the system either through family or friends or money. Without family, friends or money, you cannot enter the system. My father was in politics. My grandmother and great-grandfather were in politics. So, it was easy for me to enter politics. This is a problem. I am a symptom of this problem. I want to change it.

Right from his early days in politics, Rahul has admitted that that is the point he is trying to make. But, that has not prevented him from invoking his family and making statements like: 'I belong to a family which has never moved backwards, which has never gone back on its words. You know that when any member of my family has decided to do anything, he does it.' He said this during a roadshow in Uttar Pradesh in April 2007. The irony of a dynast speaking against dynastic politics and striving to democratize his party by putting meritocracy above everything else hasn't gone unregistered. Neither has the realization that what he has set out to do, or claims to have set out to do, is a tall order. Within the Congress, dynasty lurks in every corner. Its roots run deep; perhaps deeper than Rahul Gandhi is willing to admit.

Apart from its most prized dynast, the Party has scores of second- or third-generation politicians who have been given party tickets on the lone virtue of their being the sons or daughters of politicians. Patrick French, in his book *India: An Intimate Biography of 1.2 Billion People*, calls them HMPs, or hereditary MPs, whose lives have followed uncannily similar trajectories: early years in a boarding school; college in Europe or the United States; a stint in a bank or in some international company; and finally, 'a return to the safe family seat in the late twenties'. The minister of state for communications and information technology Sachin Pilot, who became member of Parliament at the age of twenty-six, is the son of Rajesh Pilot. The senior Pilot, who was a first-generation politician, had held a similar portfolio in the 1990s. Minister of state for commerce and industry, Jyotiraditya Madhavrao Scindia, is the son of Madhavrao Scindia who was railways minister in the Rajiv Gandhi government.

Milind Deora, the MP from Mumbai South, is the son of former union minister for petroleum and natural gas, Murli Deora, a trusted aide of the Gandhi family. The minister of state for road transport and highways, Jitin Prasada, is the son of Jitendra Prasada, who was once vice-president of the Congress Party and political adviser to Rajiv Gandhi. His grandfather, Jyoti Prasada, was also a member of the Congress Party. East Delhi MP Sandeep Dikshit's mother is Chief Minister Sheila Dikshit who has led the Congress to victory in the Delhi assembly elections thrice consecutively. Her father-in-law, Uma Shankar Dikshit, was closely associated with Jawaharlal, Indira and Rajiv. The Congress MP from Kurukshetra, Naveen Jindal, is the son of Congress leader O.P. Jindal who was minister for power in the Haryana government in 2005. The Congress MP from Rohtak, Deependra Singh Hooda, is the son of Haryana chief minister Bhupinder Singh Hooda. Other senior Congress leaders like P. Chidambaram, too, have jumped on the dynasty bandwagon. His son, Karti P. Chidambaram, is also a politician. Finance Minister Pranab Mukherjee's son, Abhijit, was elected member of the West Bengal legislative assembly on a Congress ticket within weeks of joining politics. A survey commissioned by French found that as of 2010, nearly 38 per cent of Congress

MPs had reached the Lok Sabha because of their family connections. The startling reality is that every single Congress MP under the age of thirty-five has, in a way, inherited the seat. In the thirty-one to forty age bracket, too, there are about 86 per cent HMPs. While the Congress takes the lead when it comes to dynastic politics, it is not the only party where name defines a person's position.

Political dynasties prevail across the country and in most of the political parties, barring a few exceptions like the Left parties which have, until now, succeeded in steering clear of them. Let's begin with Jammu and Kashmir where the state's largest political party, National Conference, has been a family affair of the Abdullahs who have been around for three generations. Sheikh Mohammed Abdullah was the first president of Kashmir's first political party, Muslim Conference, later renamed National Conference. When it was time to appoint a successor, he chose his son Farooq, who passed on the family legacy to his son Omar. The Opposition, the Jammu and Kashmir People's Democratic Party (PDP), hasn't been any better. Its founder, Mufti Mohammad Sayeed, was only too pleased to have his daughter, Mehbooba Mufti, succeed him as PDP president.

At the southern tip of the country, in Tamil Nadu too, dynastic politics is the norm. The state's Dravida Munnetra Kazhagam (DMK) has made politics an extended family business. DMK head M. Karunanidhi's sons, M.K. Stalin and M.K. Alagiri, are prominent leaders of the Party. So is his daughter Kanimozhi. (She was sent to jail as an undertrial in 2011 on charges of being one of the principal beneficiaries of India's biggest telecom scam.) Another political party from Tamil Nadu, Pattali Makkal Katchi (PMK), has its founder S. Ramadoss seeking a successor in his son, Anbumani Ramadoss. A similar pattern is visible in the Nationalist Congress Party (NCP). NCP president Sharad Pawar's daughter, Supriya Sule, and nephew, Ajit Pawar, are also politicians.

The two most significant political parties of Punjab, the Congress and the Akali Dal, also believe in keeping power within the family. In their case, the links aren't just linear but have spread out into the extended family. Akali Dal supremo, Parkash Singh Badal, appointed his son Sukhbir president of the Shiromani Akali Dal, bypassing several senior and more accomplished leaders in the Party. With the senior Badal as chief minister of the state, Sukhbir was made deputy chief minister. Sukhbir's wife, Harsimrat Kaur, is an MP from Bathinda. She defeated another dynast, Raninder Singh, the son of Punjab Congress leader and former chief minister Amarinder Singh and Preneet Kaur, a minister in the United Progressive Alliance (UPA) government. Parkash Singh Badal's nephew, Manpreet Badal, is also a politician and was finance minister of the state before he fell out with his uncle.

In Uttar Pradesh, Samajwadi Party president Mulayam Singh Yadav's brother, Shivpal, and son, Akhilesh, are also examples of how politics has turned into a family occupation. There are several other examples—from the Thackerays and the Chavans in Maharashtra to the Patnaiks in Orissa, the Hoodas and the Chautalas in Haryana to the Sangmas in Meghalaya. Since Independence, the number of political dynasties in India has multiplied manifold.

The Bharatiya Janata Party (BJP)—which has always lambasted its single biggest rival, the Congress, for its obsession with lineage, and takes pride in identifying itself as a democratic party—has by and large steered clear of dynasties. There are certain exceptions, though. Anurag Thakur, the MP from Hamirpur in Himachal Pradesh, is the son of BJP leader Prem Kumar Dhumal who has twice been chief minister of the hill state. The sons of senior BJP leaders Jaswant Singh and Vasundhara Raje have followed in the footsteps of their parents. Even so, the number of BJP MPs who are in the Lok Sabha because of their surname is only half that of the Congress. The Party and its ideological parent, the Rashtriya Swayamsevak Sangh (RSS), do not welcome the attempts of their leaders to push in their sons or daughters. To cite an example, when former BJP president Rajnath Singh tried to get one of his sons into politics, the move was nipped in the bud. Yet, the number of BJP leaders seeking tickets for their children increases with every election.

Expressing his anguish over the increasing concentration of power in the hands of a few hundred families, senior BJP leader Arun Jaitley said:

> Post-1991, all new political parties which have come up in India are caste-centric and personality-centric . . . Some of the older parties have also moved in that direction . . . The whole emphasis in the last two decades has been on families and succession through the family—whether it's the National Conference, Akali Dal, Samajwadi Party, etc.

In March 2011, while hitting out at Prime Minister Manmohan Singh for saying that veteran BJP leader L.K. Advani 'believed that being the prime minister was his birthright . . . and therefore he has never forgiven

me', Jaitley said, 'Democratic parties which elect
leaders on the basis of merit never accept the concept
of birthright. It [is] only parties that believe in dynastic
succession which are committed to the concept of
birthright. Members of a dynasty acquire the right to
govern as they are born into a family.'

Congressmen, however, would like to believe that
the dynastic politics of their party is different from and
more justifiable than that of the others. An average
Congressman conditions himself to believe that merit
lies only in the dynasty that runs the Congress. Mani
Shankar Aiyar, a former diplomat who quit the foreign
service to plunge into politics and join Rajiv Gandhi,
his crony from school, would obviously be expected to
defend the Gandhi clan's continued dominance over the
affairs of the Party. And this is what he had to say even
when he was down and out in the Party:

The single greatest understanding of where the
buck stops within the Party is at the Nehru–
Gandhi family. The family is the still centre
around which everything revolves and though it
is seen as a weakness by others, this is actually the
strength of the Party. They allow large freedom of
expression and large participation. There is complete

democracy except on a fundamental question like secularism.

Aiyar said these words to one of the authors of this book on his last day at 14 Akbar Road, his government-allotted minister's residence. His status as a minister was downgraded in the UPA-I regime and he was eventually dropped from the ministry. Aiyar's defence of the family, despite his having fallen out of favour, is telling. Though he was sulking at being sidelined within the Party, it did not stop him from eulogizing the Gandhis.

Stretch the canvas further and it emerges that dynasties have proved attractive not only in India but in several other South Asian countries. In Pakistan, after Benazir Bhutto's assassination, her husband Asif Ali Zardari had no trouble coming to power. Canny enough to spot political opportunity, he got his son Bilawal Zardari to add 'Bhutto' to his name and become Bilawal Zardari Bhutto. Martyrdom—the term used for political assassinations in this part of the world—is attractive. It evokes sympathy. Leaders who capture the people's imagination are idolized. And if some tragedy befalls those leaders, it's bound to sway public sentiment in favour of their families. After Benazir Bhutto's father, former Pakistan prime minister Zulfikar Ali Bhutto, was sentenced to death following a coup led by General Zia-ul-Haq, it was only natural for the people of Pakistan to welcome Benazir into politics. In Sri Lanka, Sirimavo Ratwatte Dias Bandaranaike was elected prime minister soon after the assassination of her husband, Solomon Bandaranaike, while he was in office. Later, their daughter, Chandrika Kumaratunga, became the President of Sri Lanka. In Bangladesh, Sheikh Hasina, the daughter of the country's first President, Sheikh Mujibur Rahman, became prime minister twenty years after her father was killed in a coup which involved his colleagues from the Awami League.

Rahul Gandhi is dealing with a mindset that extends beyond the boundaries of India. In such a scenario, what are the odds that he will succeed in reforming and correcting the system? Will the man who is himself a product of a deep-rooted dynasty succeed in breaking the mould for others and put merit first? Will he be able to change the culture of the Congress? Or will that culture derail his plans? How will dynasty represent modernity? The old guard within the Congress is quite effective when it comes to resisting change. The official history of the Congress speaks of how Rajiv's attempts to rid the Party of vested interests—whom he called the 'power brokers'—ran into a rock-solid wall and how his efforts to energize the Party by bringing in young blood and running it in a professional manner didn't quite achieve the success that he had hoped for.

According to Aiyar, the only person before Rahul who tried to infuse democracy within the Congress Party was Rajiv.

> Rajiv Gandhi once told me that his worst apprehension was that if the *mai baap sarkar* continued to fail to deliver, succeeding generations of young would be in danger of taking to violent means. That was his political raison d'être for emphasizing the importance of Panchayati Raj or what we today call inclusive governance. The only way of securing inclusive growth is through inclusive governance. Therefore, the Congress must become a champion of inclusive governance if it is to be seen as the standard-bearer of inclusive growth. That is the way forward. But if we come to be associated with being only the party of accelerated growth, then people will soon label us as the party of accelerated disparities; that would be the path to political disaster, not only for our party but democracy itself.

Aiyar said he was 'deeply concerned at the continuing absence of the democratic process within the Party', something that Rajiv had tried to correct.

He raised a lot of porcupine quills by targeting what he called 'brokers of power' within the Party— discrediting the Party from within. He formed the Uma Shankar Dikshit committee to democratize the organization. However, before the recommendations were operationalized, we suffered the election reverses of November 1989. He was so convinced that the only way to rejuvenate the Party was to adopt the Dikshit committee recommendations that he first convened the extended CWC [Congess Working Committee] meeting in April 1990 to endorse the Dikshit report and then the Plenary of AICC in June 1990 to ratify it.

The political situation in the country at that time and Rajiv's assassination in May 1991 ensured that the Party shelved the Dikshit report.

Twenty years later, Rahul stands at the same juncture. Aiyar said, 'The only segment of the Congress organization structure which is genuinely democratic is the NSUI [National Students' Union of India] and the IYC [Indian Youth Congress] at the insistence of General Secretary Rahul Gandhi.' For him, Rahul's formula could propel the Congress back into the dominant status it had enjoyed before the 1990s.

It is critical that the Rahul initiative be extended beyond NSUI–IYC to the Party as a whole. By a combination of democracy from within and reorienting the Party's philosophy and image to replacing the mai baap sarkar with inclusive governance, I predict with confidence that within a decade we can restore the Congress to national prominence at the Centre and in the states, but not otherwise.

On the other hand, the absence of inner party democracy could gradually weaken the Congress. In Aiyar's words, 'Like a tree, you can't have strong branches and weak roots.'

But how much can be achieved by a man who has stepped into politics at his age? Rahul was already thirty-three when he came into politics. Going by India's life expectancy, that's about half a lifetime. He has said that he made up his mind to enter politics the day his father died.

I took the decision when I was in the train with my father's body [ashes] coming to Allahabad. Coincidentally, it was as we entered UP. I looked out of the train and I saw a lot of people following. And in their faces I saw a sense of loss and I felt that as my father's son I had some responsibility.

Yet, it took him thirteen years to finally take the first step towards fulfilling that 'responsibility'. He waited for over a decade to begin his education and do the groundwork that would equip him to understand the complexities of Indian politics. Motilal was twenty-seven when he attended the first Congress meeting, and Jawaharlal's political innings began around the same age, though some members of the Nehru–Gandhi family have indeed been late entrants into politics. When Indira became Congress president, she was forty-two. While Sanjay was barely thirty when he stood for elections, Rajiv was thirty-six when he entered politics.

Rahul was hardly a boy when he stepped into politics, but he continued to be treated as one even after the age of forty. During an interview in November 2008, when he was asked by Shekhar Gupta of the *Indian Express* what he thought of Rahul Gandhi, the then-BJP president Rajnath Singh, who was in his mid-fifties, quipped, 'I consider Rahul a *bachcha* [child], so I would not want to say anything about him.' A few days later, Rahul hit back. He said, 'I am a bachcha but the fortunate, or unfortunate, thing is, 70 per cent of this country is also bachcha.' This wasn't the first time the BJP had called him a kid, implying that he was a political novice and not to be taken too seriously. Before him, Rajiv

Gandhi's cabinet had been labelled *babalog*. The same term is frequently used by the opposition parties to mock the young parliamentarians now led by Rahul. During a verbal duel between Rahul and V.S. Achuthanandan, then the chief minister of Kerala, in the run-up to the 2011 assembly elections in the state, age became the flashpoint. 'If the LDF [Left Democratic Front] is re-elected, Kerala will have a ninety-three-year-old as chief minister in five years' time,' Rahul said in April 2011. A day later, Achuthanandan hit back by calling him 'Amul Baby'. He said, 'I need not tell you that Rahul Gandhi is Sonia Gandhi's son. He has launched a large number of Amul Babies as Congress candidates.'

It's a clash of generations. While on one hand, the youth brigade is finding its feet in politics, on the other hand, the old brigade is still calling the shots. In Indian politics, youth is equated with naivety. Given that the average age of the Indian political leader is well past fifty, it's not difficult to understand why. When Rahul entered politics, Prime Minister Manmohan Singh was already seventy-one, Pranab Mukherjee was sixty-eight and P. Chidambaram was fifty-eight. Opposition leaders, too, were getting on in age. L.K. Advani was seventy-six, Sushma Swaraj had already touched fifty-two and Arun Jaitley was fifty-one.

What's interesting is how Congressmen throw their weight behind the Gandhis, especially Rahul, every time the family faces a challenge from opponents. When Achuthanandan called Rahul 'Amul Baby', stalwarts like Pranab Mukherjee jumped to his defence and termed the open attack as 'uncivilized'. Congress spokesperson Abhishek Manu Singhvi also lashed out, 'It's an insult to the entire youth of the country who, in this millennium, are resurgent. This comment is an insult to the momentum of youth power. The Congress has a youth icon and youth symbol in Rahul Gandhi, which no other party has.'

When the Bihar assembly results came out in 2010 and it emerged that Rahul's formula of doing away with alliances had boomeranged on the Party, Congressmen again formed a protective ring around the family, and, as always, took the brickbats for the mistakes and the failures. In times such as these, the family which owes its political existence to the Party is immediately placed on a pedestal while the Party takes the flak. In the case of Rahul Gandhi, the Party will not allow anyone to damage his image.

Another dynast from the family, however, hasn't had it this easy. Indira's other and lesser-known grandson, Feroze Varun Gandhi, stands at the other end of the political and ideological spectrum. Though a direct descendant of the Nehru–Gandhi family, Varun, who is Sanjay and Maneka's son, has opted for the BJP, the party to which his mother belongs. Rahul and Varun make for starkly contrasting case studies. While one cousin is openly celebrated by his party as its next prime ministerial candidate, the other often stands practically isolated within his party. To a large extent, it boils down to the choices which Rahul and Varun and their fathers or mothers have made. While Rajiv enjoyed the goodwill of the people, Sanjay was almost hated for his policies. While Rahul makes an extra effort to be seen as secular, Varun has done just the opposite. While the Congress would like nothing better than to see Rahul as prime minister of India, the BJP remains distrustful of Varun because he is, at the end of the day, a Gandhi. BJP leaders have often pulled up Varun for his deviation from the party line. In Rahul's case, any variance becomes the new party line.

Speaking to students at Aligarh Muslim University in December 2009, Rahul said:

You need to step up and the number of leaders coming out of your community needs to go up. Today, you have a Sikh prime minister. Nobody would have ever imagined in a country of over a billion people that we would have a Sikh prime minister. Sikhs are a very small percentage of this country.

Compare that to Varun who, before his first parliamentary elections in 2009, had targeted the community. To the nation's outrage, he was seen on camera launching a venomous attack on Muslims during an election campaign in his constituency, Pilibhit, Uttar Pradesh. His party, the BJP, makes no pretence of being secular but Varun had played the communal card to an embarrassing extreme. The BJP immediately distanced itself from his hate speech.

Rahul, too, has made his share of controversial statements, like those on the demolition of the Babri Masjid and the making of Bangladesh. But his party has always stood by him. And though he detests being called '*yuvraj*' or heir apparent, that's the treatment he gets from the Congress. Many view Manmohan Singh as a caretaker who will happily hand over the prime minister's chair once Rahul is ready.

Despite the initial advantage, Rahul appears to have chosen to go the hard way. Though he comes across as a well-meaning politician, the question is: Will that be enough? His father was also well-meaning but he couldn't get very far when he tried to transform the grand old party into a professional organization. Rahul is a keen learner and evidently wants to have a good grasp over his subject—Indian politics. But at some stage, he will also have to become a leader. In October 2008, during a visit to Dehradun in Uttarakhand, he was asked whether the democratization process which he had put in place for NSUI and IYC elections would apply to the internal elections in the Congress Working Committee and for the post of Congress president. Rahul was non-committal: 'I am general secretary in charge of the Youth Congress. My jurisdiction ends with the Youth Congress and the NSUI. That is where my work is.' Three years later, not much seemed to have changed. As prime-minister-in-waiting, he will need to look and think beyond the Youth Congress and the NSUI. With India emerging as a global power, can he afford to restrict his politics to the Party's youth wings and Uttar Pradesh, which he calls his 'karmabhoomi'? At some stage, he will have to show the qualities needed in a national and a global leader, like his grandmother.

In 1966, when Indira was made prime minister of India, socialist Ram Manohar Lohia had called her a gungi gudiya (dumb doll). Senior Congress leaders had expected her to be the perfect prop, a compliant prime minister who would do as told. How wrong their judgement proved to be! As she threw herself into politics, Indira showed that she was anything but dumb and soon earned the title of 'Iron Lady'. For Rahul, too, these are early days. We know where he is coming from; it is where he is headed that matters. Will he show the same political acumen as his grandmother and great-grandfather? Or, will he continue to be a well-intentioned learner performing only under test conditions?

The Inevitable:
Death and Politics

3 November 1984. Prime Minister Indira Gandhi's body lay in state at Teen Murti Bhavan, a colonial-era building that had once been her father Jawaharlal Nehru's home. She was India's first woman prime minister and before she was shot dead on 31 October 1984, she had been the head of the world's largest democracy four times over. The nation was in mourning. Standing to the right of Indira's body was a fourteen-year-old boy, also in mourning. The events of the last few days had rocked his life in more ways than he was probably aware of at that point of time. Rahul stood there, his gaze intent on

Indira's face. Then, he carefully wiped the dead prime minister's cheek. That brief display of emotion in public was but a momentary glimpse of the bond which Indira and Rahul had shared.

Later in the day, Rahul walked a step ahead of his father, Rajiv, who had by then been sworn in as prime minister of India. Occasionally, he would turn back to look at his father or touch the plank on which Indira's body rested—a plank that Rajiv supported on his right shoulder. At Shakti Sthal, Indira's final resting place, Rahul stood almost hidden behind the flames that consumed his grandmother's body as leaders from across the world who had gathered for the funeral watched. In many ways, Indira was the one who shaped Rahul's destiny. From the time he was born till her death, she stayed closely involved with him. It was she who had named him Rahul. Family and friends say that Indira doted on her first grandchild. In a letter to her friend Dorothy Norman soon after his birth on 19 June 1970, she wrote, 'My grandson Rahul is a darling. He has got rid of his wrinkles and still has his double chin!' Though her work day as prime minister was packed, she would try to steal time to be with him in the morning before starting work, and would often look him up before going to sleep. Frank writes that, as toddlers,

Rahul and Priyanka would sometimes accompany Indira to her morning darshans when she met hoards of admirers in her garden. And, she would often have them sleep in her room at night in order to be with them.

Indira confided in Rahul as she rarely did in anyone else. With him, she even shared her fear of being assassinated. 'After Operation Blue Star, my mother-in-law knew that she was going to be killed. She knew that her days were numbered. She spoke to my son in particular about it,' Sonia said in a television interview soon after taking over as Congress president.

Rahul was not at home the morning his grandmother was killed. It was on a Wednesday and at 9.08 a.m. He and Priyanka were both at school. The *Indian Express* reported that, during his visit to Kashmir University in Srinagar in September 2011, Rahul told students:

I was sitting inside the classroom looking out of a window and suddenly, someone came into the classroom and the teacher stopped teaching. He shared something with the teacher and asked me to come to [the] principal's room. A woman, on phone, told me to reach home immediately. My grandmother had been killed.

As a frantic Sonia rushed the blood-soaked Indira in an Ambassador car to the All India Institute of Medical Sciences (AIIMS) with the prime minister's aide, R.K. Dhawan, a team of the Delhi police rushed to Rahul's school in the heart of the city. On the face of it, it seemed the police team was taking him to AIIMS, but a smaller squad quietly took him home to 1 Safdarjung Road.

Indira's conviction that she would be killed or that her family would come to harm had already affected the lives of those around her, especially that of Rahul. She had become paranoid about the possible danger to his life. In 1981, Rahul had left to study at Doon, a school situated in an idyllic valley nestled between the Garhwal Himalayas and the hills of Shivalik. Rajiv, too, had been to the same school. But in 1983, barely two years after he had enrolled, Rahul had been plucked from that peaceful life and brought back to Delhi. Indira worried too much about his safety, and wanted him and Priyanka by her side. Punjab was on the boil and she knew that the decisions she had taken in the past could well blow up in her face. She feared that someone might kidnap the children to get back at her. In her final months, Indira had also told Rahul and Priyanka not to play outside the gate that separated the garden of their residence, 1 Safdarjung Road, from the path that led to her office.

Indira tried to spend as much time as she could with her grandchildren. On 27 October 1984, four days before she was killed, she took a break from work and went to Srinagar on a day-long trip with Rahul and Priyanka. Two days later, she was off to Bhubaneswar, the capital of Orissa, where she gave her final speech, clearly alluding to the death which she was convinced was imminent: 'I am here today, I may not be here tomorrow . . . I shall continue to serve until my last breath and when I die, I can say that every drop of my blood will invigorate India and strengthen it.'

Later that evening, when she returned to Raj Bhavan where she was staying, she got a phone call from Delhi. Rahul and Priyanka's car had met with a minor accident while bringing them back from school. The children, she was told, were unhurt, but Indira wanted to see that for herself. She cut short her Orissa trip and flew back to Delhi the same night. Rahul and Priyanka were asleep by the time she reached home. She retired to her room only after Sonia assured her that the children were fine. It would turn out to be the last night of Indira's life.

***

Rahul's birth had cemented Indira's relationship with Sonia. A year before he was born, Sonia had suffered a miscarriage. In those days, Indira was learning yoga at her residence from Dhirendra Brahmachari, a bearded, long-haired swami who later went on to become a key figure in her life. But Sonia was not quite comfortable with yoga during her first pregnancy and, to some extent, blamed Indira's obsession with it for the miscarriage, writes journalist Rasheed Kidwai in his book *Sonia: A Biography*. Rahul's arrival acted as a balm, bringing his mother and grandmother closer. Between the two of them, Sonia and Indira had defined their roles very well. There was no room for conflict. Indira ran the country. Sonia ran the household. It was a choice they had made for themselves.

Rahul's mother was not into politics. Nor was his father. At least, not yet. Though his grandmother was one of the world's most powerful political leaders of the time, Rahul's parents had chosen a life sheltered from public glare. Sonia was born to Italian parents on 9 December 1946, near Lusiana, a small town in northern Italy. She grew up as Edvige Antonia Albina Maino in a traditional Roman Catholic family and, in 1964, went to Cambridge to study English. It was here that she met her future husband, Rajiv, in a Greek restaurant. At that point of time, Sonia had only a faint idea of Rajiv's political lineage. For Rajiv, too, his political background was incidental. He had no intention of letting it define his future. Instead of following in his mother's footsteps, he chose to become a commercial pilot. As Captain Rajiv Gandhi, he flew the Avro 748 aircraft for the Indian Airlines between Delhi, Agra and Jaipur. It was his first airliner before he graduated to the Boeing. The Avro 748 was a rather uncomfortable plane to fly. Its interiors got unbearably hot in summer. The cramped seating space caused inconvenience to passengers. The cabin air conditioning was far from ideal. For those who could afford to pay for a more comfortable flight, the Avro 748 was clearly not the first choice. Rahul's father too did not enjoy flying the Avro 748, but he preferred it to politics. An air crash, however, changed the course of his journey and sucked him and his family into the life which they had tried to steer clear of.

On the morning of 23 June 1980—four days after Rahul's tenth birthday—Rajiv's younger brother, Sanjay, died in an air crash near Safdarjung Airport in New Delhi. He was trying to perform an aerobatic loop in his new Pitts S-2A, a two-seater plane, when he lost control. The plane nosedived into the ground, killing Sanjay and his instructor, Captain Subhash Saxena. Indira's politically ambitious son died instantaneously. Sanjay had been Indira's adviser and the person to whom she turned when faced with a political dilemma. He was the one who had got her to impose the Emergency in 1975—a move that cost Indira her prime ministership in the elections held two years later. The Emergency, remembered as the darkest period in Indian democracy, forced unprecedented restrictions on the freedom of expression and gagged the press, the critical fourth pillar of democracy. It saw Sanjay and his team—'Sanjay's Action Brigade'—imposing forced sterilization on men as the ideal way to check population explosion and, in the name of beautification, razing slums to the ground and moving slum-dwellers to the fringes of the city. Amnesty International reported that during the first year of Emergency over one lakh people were arrested and kept in jails without trial. Among those arrested were J.P. Narayan, Gayatri Devi of Jaipur and Morarji Desai. Sanjay's idea of Emergency violated the very tenets of democracy. It eventually left Indira jobless and without a source of income for the first time in her life when India rose to give its mandate against her in the 1977 general elections.

The defeat forced Indira to move out of her Safdarjung residence to a much smaller house, 12

Willingdon Crescent, which belonged to Mohammad Yunus, an old friend of the Nehru–Gandhi family. He had vacated it for them. It was here that Rahul's mother and grandmother began to truly trust each other. As Sonia took complete charge of the house—from cooking the vegetables which she had grown in the kitchen garden to planning important dinners—Indira came to rely more and more on her. After her defeat, Indira had become exceedingly cautious about the people around her. With Sonia stepping forward to take control, at least one aspect of Indira's life remained by and large undisturbed, and she could focus on her work. She set about doing what needed to be done to regain power. Her prime ministership gone, Indira now had more time on hand than she had had in years, and she spent a lot of it with her two grandchildren—Rahul and Priyanka. Her bond with her older son's family grew.

While her political career was going through an upheaval, it was not entirely peaceful at home, either. Though Rajiv didn't care much for politics, he did care about the situation in which his mother found herself due to Sanjay's doings. Despite the many arguments between Rahul's father and uncle on the issue, Sanjay's death left a huge void. Even though his ways were anti-democratic and his policies skewed, the fact was that Sanjay had been

Indira's political heir. His death left her shattered. Rajiv and Sonia were in Italy with the children when the accident took place. They rushed back to be at Indira's side. Sonia later described that Indira 'for all her courage and composure, was broken in spirit'. She was a picture of despair as she walked up to Sanjay's samadhi to pay homage, flowers in hand, wearing a white sari draped over her head. Indira still had the fire in her, but the recent storm had left the flames flickering. She was terrified of losing her second son, the pilot. An air crash had claimed her younger one, and now she was scared to let the older one fly.

The focus turned to Rajiv. Indira desperately wanted him by her side. Pressure mounted on him, not just from his mother but also from loyalists within the Congress. Sonia revealed that Rajiv was 'tormented by the conflict'. In an interview in the documentary, *India's Rajiv*, directed by Simi Garewal, Rajiv said, 'I was never interested in politics or a public life. I just wanted to be out of it.' He said he wanted to be himself, alone, the way it was when he was flying. 'We had a little family and we were all very happy. With my brother's accident, things changed. My mother needed help. She felt that she couldn't get it from anywhere, except from me.'

Years after Rajiv's death, Sonia spoke of how she had 'fought like a tigress for our life together'. It was a tough decision but in the end Indira had her way. Sonia, though uncomfortable with his decision to enter politics, stood by Rajiv. 'We had very long talks, my wife and I, before I gave up flying and joined politics,' he said in *India's Rajiv*. 'She was not too happy about it, mainly because she felt that in a sense she would be losing me. I think that was the crux of the issue.' Ten months after Sanjay's death, Rahul's father announced that he would stand for by-elections from Amethi, formerly his brother's constituency. On 10 May 1981, Indian Airlines accepted Rajiv's resignation. The next day, he filed his nomination. With that, his chapter as a pilot ended and so did the private life he had so carefully planned for his family. It was only a matter of time before his wife and children would also find themselves in the rough and tumble of Indian politics.

Sonia wasn't the only one who questioned Rajiv's decision to enter politics. In a press briefing, Rahul recalled an incident when he was campaigning with his father. Both father and son had been on the go for days, trying to woo voters. The campaign was to end in four or five days. The last few days had been long and demanding, and both of them were exhausted.

We were walking up the stairs of the plane when I asked my father, 'Papa, why do you do this? Have you ever thought that you should leave this?' My father looked at me, surprised, and I asked again, 'What is this? You didn't want to do this in the first place. You wanted to be a pilot. Have you ever thought about leaving it?'

Rajiv's wife and children were clearly not comfortable with his being in politics. Indira's death had only drawn him deeper into it. Within hours of his mother's assassination at the hands of her bodyguards, Rajiv was pressed by top Congress leaders to take over as prime minister of India. This time, Rajiv did not wait to take a decision the way he had done when Sanjay died. Sonia—who had taken Indira's bloodied body, punctured by thirty bullets, to AIIMS that morning—was completely shaken when her husband told her that he was taking up the job. The assassins had fired thirty-one bullets at Indira, of which thirty had hit her. Twenty-three bullets had passed through her body and the remaining seven were trapped inside. These ghastly details would emerge only later. Standing in the hospital, Sonia didn't know these facts yet. What she did know, however, was that her mother-in-law had been brutally killed and her husband, who had never imagined a life in politics, was going to step into her shoes.

P.C. Alexander, former principal secretary to Rajiv Gandhi, later wrote that he had accidentally walked into a room at AIIMS and found Rajiv hugging Sonia. He heard him telling Sonia that he had to take the job and Sonia begging him not to. 'I did not want my husband to become prime minister,' Sonia said in subsequent interviews. 'I was literally begging him not to. I told him that I didn't want him to do it because he would be killed. And my husband answered, "I would be killed in any case."'

Rahul's father, the man who wanted to have nothing to do with politics, went on to become the seventh prime minister of India. At the age of forty, with only about three and a half years of political experience, he was also the youngest to hold the post. By the age of forty, Rahul would have double that experience in active politics and would be firmly evading questions about the possibility of his becoming prime minister of the country. But for Rajiv, everything happened as though in fast-track mode. Soon after taking over as prime minister, he led the Congress Party to an astounding victory, riding on the sympathy wave that swept the nation after Indira's death. The Congress won 411 out of 542 seats—the largest majority ever in Indian Parliament.

Veteran Congressmen who had feared that the Party would be left leaderless after Indira, found the perfect candidate in Rajiv. He had a future-oriented approach and, with the kind of numbers he had on his side, it was just all that easier for him to try and bring about the changes he desired and to make serious mistakes. One of the changes he brought about was to modernize the telecommunications industry and connect every part of the country through telephones. In a way, he set the stage for the cell phone revolution which transformed the way India connected with itself and the outside world. India was still a very young democracy when Rajiv became prime minister. It was only thirty-seven years since the country achieved independence after nearly two centuries of British rule. There was an immense amount of work to be done. And the young prime minister, who was brimming with ideas, wanted nothing short of a transformation. He wanted to overhaul the way things had been functioning for decades under the Licence Raj. As he became more and more involved with work, his time with Rahul and Priyanka became limited and this bothered him. 'If anybody has really had to sacrifice, it's been the children,' he once said.

Sonia's constant fear that something terrible might happen to her husband was also shared by her children. Rahul who, in later years, would occasionally accompany his father during campaigning, said, 'In those days I also felt it was dangerous for him, but that was my personal view.' In public, Rahul's mother tried to conceal her anxiety but wasn't quite successful. She would be seen standing beside Rajiv, beautiful but aloof. On a particularly cold winter morning of January 1988, when she arrived with Rajiv to attend a Republic Day event in Delhi, her long hair neatly tied back, people remarked how rarely she smiled. Some ten years later, when journalist Vir Sanghvi asked her about this impression people had of her, Sonia reasoned that was probably because 'she was very often tense'. She said she was traumatized for a long time by Indira's assassination, and 'was always worried that something may happen to my husband'. Together, Rajiv and Sonia prepared their children for any such eventuality and also drafted identical funeral instructions for themselves. Rajiv wrote:

In the event of my death as well as that of my wife, Sonia, at or about the same time, at the same place or at different places, within or outside India, our bodies should be brought to Delhi and cremated together, in accordance with Hindu rites, in an open ground. In no circumstances should our bodies be burnt in a crematorium. According to our custom, our eldest child Rahul should light the pyre. It is my wish that our ashes should be immersed in the Ganga at Triveni, Allahabad, where my ancestors' ashes have been immersed.

As time passed, the sympathy wave which had elevated Rajiv to the prime minister's position began to ebb and he faced reality checks on various issues. One of them was the Indo-Sri Lanka Peace Accord which he signed with Sri Lankan President J.R. Jayawardene on 29 July 1987, to help resolve the ethnic conflict in the island nation south of India. Years of conflict between the Sinhalas and the Tamils of Sri Lanka had snowballed into a bloody civil war. The Tamil separatists, predominantly the Liberation Tigers of Tamil Eelam (LTTE), had found a safe haven in the south Indian state of Tamil Nadu. The peace accord between India and Sri Lanka spelt trouble for them. Under the agreement, India would send troops—the Indian Peace Keeping Force—into the country to get the LTTE to give up arms. The move antagonized both the Sinhalas, who did not want another country intervening in what they considered to be their internal matter, and the Tamil separatists, who had always believed that India was on their side. On 30 July 1987, the day after the accord was signed, Rajiv was assaulted on the head with a rifle butt while receiving the guard of honour. The assailant was a young Sinhala cadet called Vijayamunige Rohana de Silva. Rajiv ducked in time and escaped unhurt. But this open assault had driven the message home. Two years after the agreement was signed, India started withdrawing the peacekeeping force from Sri Lanka. More than a thousand Indian soldiers had died in a conflict that was not theirs and in an alien country. India had lost more than it had achieved. The bitter civil war in Sri Lanka continued.

These events did not help Rajiv's reputation. The controversial Bofors gun deal—a major corruption scandal in which several top politicians and defence officials were suspected to have received kickbacks from the Swedish armaments company—further damaged Rajiv's corruption-free 'Mr Clean' image. At the time the Bofors deal was sealed, Rajiv was handling the defence portfolio. The government went into an overdrive in its attempt to control the damage, from raiding the offices of the *Indian Express*, where the news story had first appeared, to issuing denials that only added to the suspicion. Pushed for answers, an otherwise-genial Rajiv exhibited bursts of temper. *India Today* reported in its issue of 15 November 1989 that, on one occasion, when Rajiv was asked why he hadn't responded to the Opposition's charges, he shot back, 'Am I expected to reply to every dog that barks?' As the government's credibility took a blow, the Congress found itself staring at disaster in the elections held in November that year. The Party, which had come home with a thumping majority in 1984 under Rajiv, got only 197 seats this time around. The Congress lost the elections and Rajiv, his prime ministership.

As Rajiv struggled to regain his space in power, Rahul, who was now nineteen years old, joined him on the campaign trail. He toured the country with him, going from town to town, village to village. Sonia, along with Priyanka, focussed on Amethi. Though nine years had passed since he first stepped into politics, she still worried about her husband's safety. A retired colonel of the Indian Army recalled an incident that took place in early 1991 when Rajiv was visiting the Counter Insurgency and Jungle Warfare School at Warangte in Mizoram. From there, he was to fly to Manipur. 'Rajiv had just left after meeting the officers at Warangte when there was a call from Delhi,' recollected the officer who took that call. 'Seconds after the operator put me on hold, I heard the anxious voice of a lady ask, "Where is my husband?"' It didn't take the officer long to realize that 'it was Mrs Gandhi'. He told her that Rajiv had just taken off for Manipur and then heard the click of the receiver being put down. 'That's all she wanted to know, that he was fine,' said the officer.

From the time Rajiv stepped into politics, Sonia lived in fear. It was visible on her face and evident in her voice. On 21 May 1991, her worst fears came true. Rajiv Gandhi was assassinated during a public meeting at Sriperumbudur, a village about 40 kilometres from the city of Chennai. The LTTE had taken its revenge. The dynamic young leader, the reluctant politician, was dead. It was only a matter of time before the baton would be passed on to yet another reluctant candidate, his wife Sonia, and later, to their son, Rahul.

Sonia to Rahul via Priyanka

Sonia's residence was abuzz with activity. Every face wore a smile, every eye twinkled with joy. 24 September 2007 found 10 Janpath in the grip of frenzied excitement. Jubilant Congressmen and Congresswomen made a beeline for the rectangular lawn concealed from the busy party office by a high wall. Among the first leaders from outside Delhi to reach the most powerful address in the country was the chief minister of neighbouring Haryana, Bhupinder Singh Hooda. He came with a bouquet of flowers and a bunch of ministers and MLAs in tow. By then, scores of party workers were already standing behind the railing which ran along three sides of the lawn, eagerly waiting for Sonia, and Rahul, the man of the moment, to make an appearance. It was late in the afternoon and the day was warm, but nobody seemed to mind the heat. Finally, a beaming Sonia appeared from inside the house, Rahul by her side. A thrill went through the crowd. Practically holding Rahul by the arm, Sonia walked briskly into the waiting crowd, the smile not leaving her face even for a second. Dressed in a simple black salwar suit and white dupatta, Sonia stood next to Rahul as supporters from all ranks greeted him. At times, she placed her hand on his shoulder. At other times, she guided him across to meet those on the other side of the lawn. That September afternoon, Congress president Sonia Gandhi was like a mother whose son had passed a prestigious exam or won a coveted award. The big event was Rahul's appointment as general secretary of the Congress. And Sonia, the woman who had 'fought like a tigress' to keep her husband Rajiv out of politics, was thrilled to see her son in the position his father had occupied in the early 1980s. A mother's pride had replaced the wife's fears.

Rahul was given charge of the Party's youth wing, the Indian Youth Congress, and the student wing, the National Students' Union of India. He was thirty-seven years old and had been in politics for three years as an

MP from Amethi—the constituency which his father and, later, his mother had occupied. In the initial years after Rajiv's death, not many had expected Rahul to take the plunge. His decision to leave the country for higher studies, and then to stay abroad to work, added to the impression that the older Gandhi sibling was not keen on politics. Many Congressmen had viewed Priyanka, and not Rahul, as the natural successor who would one day lead the Party, following in the footsteps of Indira. Right from her childhood, Priyanka had appeared cut out for politics. Though she was only twelve when her grandmother was assassinated, those who saw her at the funeral soon began calling her the future Indira. There was something about her that made her stand out— a visible strength, a personality that immediately inspired confidence—and heightened the resemblance to Indira. Priyanka, the younger sibling, appeared older than Rahul. And it wasn't just because she stood a head taller than him. As time would show, she was a natural when it came to interacting with people. When she finally did descend on the political arena, albeit as a campaigner and not a candidate, she appeared more accessible than Rahul. She was clearly in her element campaigning in the hot and dusty lanes of Amethi and Rae Bareli, constituencies which have become synonymous with the Gandhi family.

Compared to her, Rahul was seen as inexperienced. That perception was not without reason. Priyanka was a familiar face in politics long before Rahul made his first foray. Even in the most trying of times, she had shown the kind of mettle which is rare in someone so young.

When Rajiv was killed in 1991, Rahul was in the United States where he was studying. Sonia was too distraught to deal with anything. The responsibility of taking care of her mother and overseeing the funeral arrangements till her brother arrived from the US fell upon Priyanka. She took charge of the situation. She stood as a wall between her mother and everybody else, refusing access to Sonia's room. It was she who asked her father's friend, Satish Sharma, to arrange for her and Sonia to fly to Madras to bring Rajiv's body back to Delhi. And, it was she who went to receive Rahul when he returned to India on being informed of his father's death.

Within the Party, Rajiv's death had raised a leadership crisis. But it didn't take the Congress long to decide whom it wanted as his successor. By the afternoon of 22 May, within twenty-four hours of the assassination, the CWC decided it would call upon Sonia to become party president. Though Sonia issued a letter saying that, while she was deeply touched by the offer, she could not accept the position, the clamour for her to take charge refused to die. On 11 September, when the Election Commission announced the by-election to the Amethi seat left vacant by Rajiv's death, the 'Sonia *lao*' campaigners brought up her name again. While Rahul and Priyanka both backed Sonia's decision to stay out of politics, Priyanka was more vocal and critical of those trying to drag her mother into it. 'We have had enough of politics,' she lashed out. But politics, and the Congress, hadn't had enough of them.

After Rajiv's death, the family pulled back from politics but didn't really pull out. Though Sonia might have wanted to stay away from active politics then, she was also determined to keep Rajiv's legacy alive. Initially, she thought she could do so through the Rajiv Gandhi Foundation which was set up on 21 June 1991—exactly a month after Rajiv's death—to work in areas like science and technology, as well as literacy and health, aimed particularly at women and children. Priyanka became the force behind the foundation's projects. The government, now led by Prime Minister P.V. Narasimha Rao, helped by treating every project under the Rajiv Gandhi Foundation as a priority. But Sonia's relationship with Rao didn't stay smooth for long. After a comfortable beginning, a niggling sense of distrust took root, and the feeling was nurtured by the people around them. Within the Congress, there were leaders loyal to Rao and there were leaders loyal to Sonia. And then there were those waiting and watching to see on which side the scales would tilt. In a sense, the Congress now had two camps. One of them functioned from outside the Party, from 10 Janpath, the house to which the family had moved in February 1990 after Rajiv was ousted as prime minister. It was here that disgruntled members of the Party went to air their grievances against the Rao government. Here, they were always given a patient hearing. It wasn't long before Sonia's residence turned into a parallel power centre. Perhaps, the more powerful of the two.

After Rajiv's death, Sonia, who had always been wary of politics, chose not to shut it out of 10 Janpath. But she stayed away from what was once her husband's constituency, Amethi, till four years after his death. In those four years, things went from bad to worse in the Congress. Factionalism and discontent among party leaders and party workers grew. And so did Sonia's impatience with the investigation into her husband's death. It was widely believed that the LTTE was behind Rajiv's killing. But there were several other theories also floating around. Nothing much seemed to be coming out of the investigation even though two commissions had been set up to probe the killing.

The Justice J.S. Verma Commission looked into the lapses that had led to Rajiv's assassination. And the Justice M.C. Jain Commission probed the conspiracy angle. Both Rahul and Priyanka attended the hearings of the commissions. Priyanka, who had stayed back in India while Rahul left the country to study, was a more frequent visitor than her brother at Vigyan Bhavan where the hearings were held. She was the one who accompanied her mother to Amethi on 24 August 1995, when Sonia openly took on the Narasimha Rao government for the tardy pace of the investigation into Rajiv's assassination. Sonia was a bit nervous as she spoke to the people of Amethi for the first time after her husband's death. But Priyanka was in her element, smiling brightly and waving cheerfully to the crowd, clearly delighted by the attention her mother was getting. That day at Amethi, Sonia also spoke about the division within the Party. A year later, the friction cost the Congress an election.

The Congress Party's defeat in the 1996 general elections saw an OBC (Other Backward Classes) leader from Karnataka, H.D. Deve Gowda, emerge as prime minister, and a newly created United Front government come into power. But Deve Gowda's term as prime minister didn't last long. The Congress, which was supporting the United Front from outside, withdrew support less than a year after the government was formed. Soon after, on 21 April 1997, another United Front government, now with Janata Dal leader I.K. Gujral as prime minister, came into power. Again, the Congress lent support from outside. And again, in less than a year, the Congress pulled the plug. This time, it did so after it was found that the Jain Commission, which had been investigating the conspiracy behind Rajiv's assassination, had indicted the DMK and named it an LTTE supporter. The Congress wanted ministers from the DMK, which was part of the United Front government, dropped. Gujral refused their demand and the Congress withdrew support.

Those were years of political instability for the country. Rao's was the last regime that survived a full term. The era of coalitions was dawning on the Indian political scene. It had to go through a phase of volatility, though, before another government would run a full term. But a greater instability existed within the Congress. The grand old party that had been credited with winning one battle after the other since 1885 was now at war with itself. Leaders big and small—including those who were products of the chaos—were pulling the Party in different directions. It was in the midst of, and perhaps because of, these mutinies within the Party that Sonia entered the scene. She decided to campaign for the Party. Her arrival was formally announced on 28 December 1997—the 112th anniversary of the Indian National Congress. As always, Sonia took the decision only after consulting her children, Rahul and Priyanka. 'She felt it was her duty to do so,' Priyanka said many years later, speaking of her mother's plunge into politics. Sonia also said that she felt she was being 'very cowardly to sit there and watch the Party go in such a bad way'. She said in a television interview that she owed it to the family 'which had lived, and died practically, for the Congress Party'.

As enthused Congressmen got down to planning Sonia's first public meeting, it was Priyanka who was constantly by her side, lending her the much-needed moral and emotional support. On 11 January 1998, when Sonia made her debut as a Congress campaigner at Sriperumbudur—the town where a suicide bomber had killed Rajiv seven years earlier—Priyanka accompanied her. It was a poignant moment for mother and daughter. The crowd was mesmerized by Priyanka whose presence was as electrifying as the vibrant red and saffron sari she wore. She spoke just one sentence in Tamil, asking the people to vote for the Congress, and it sent the crowd into raptures. The Congress instantly knew it had found its star campaigner. The Party was thrilled. Wherever she went, the impact of Priyanka's presence was the same. Some weeks later in Ranchi, now the capital of the new state of Jharkhand but then a district in the southern part of Bihar, her hand-waving eclipsed Sonia's eight-minute speech in Hindi. About 20,000 people had turned up for the rally, mostly for a glimpse of the mother and the daughter.

Sonia–Priyanka rallies were big crowd-pullers but did not prove good enough to counter the saffron wave triggered by the Ram Janmabhoomi temple movement. The Gandhi–Nehru clan's re-emergence in active politics couldn't quite get the Party the numbers that the Congress needed for its fortunes to turn. Instead, the BJP-led National Democratic Alliance (NDA) came to power. Atal Bihari Vajpayee became prime minister of India and Sonia took over the reins of the Congress. She had been made Congress president in March 1998. The NDA, however, had a wafer-thin majority which it lost in the fourteenth month when Tamil actor-turned-politician J. Jayalalithaa's party, All India Anna Dravida Munnetra Kazhagam (AIADMK), withdrew support. The country faced another general election, and Sonia, another litmus test.

The losses of the last elections had been blamed on the earlier Congress president, Sitaram Kesri. But the 1999 elections would be different. Victory or defeat, this time, it would be Sonia who would wear the crown or shoulder the blame. Again, it was Priyanka who went all out to help Sonia as she took on this formidable challenge. Priyanka, who had written all her mother's speeches during her first campaign, accompanied her once again on the campaign trail. Rahul also took leave from his job abroad to be by his mother's side at this critical time. The spotlight, though, was clearly on Priyanka who campaigned aggressively for Sonia while Rahul lent his mother moral support.

Priyanka's charisma rattled even the senior leaders in the BJP. Her first speech of the season was at Siruguppa, a town in the Bellary district of Karnataka. The person pitched against her mother was BJP stalwart Sushma Swaraj, a strong and formidable orator. The BJP had decided to go hammer and tongs, at Sonia's Italian roots. As planned, Sushma, too, played Sonia's 'foreign origin' card during her election rally at Bellary. Her appeal in Kannada to the people was, '*Swadeshi naarige puraskara, videshi naarige tiraskara* (Reward the Indian woman, reject the foreigner).' The result at Bellary could have been different had Priyanka not arrived on the scene. Days before the campaigning ended, Priyanka landed in Bellary, and Sushma knew she had lost the seat to Sonia. Priyanka chose not to target the BJP or counter its target-Sonia's-foreign-origin campaign. Instead, she made a brief appeal for her mother in Kannada that hit a chord: '*Bellariya nanna preethiya akka thangiyare, ivattu nanna thayiyannu nimmalige kare thandiruve. Ivaru nimmavaru. Ivarannu neevu yella reethiyalli rakshishi gellisi kodobeku* (Dear sisters of Bellary, I have brought my mother to you today. You must take care of her and ensure her victory).' Later in the evening, she accompanied Sonia in an open-top vehicle through the streets of Bellary, waving and smiling. By the end of the day, the mood at Bellary said it all. Victory was already Sonia's.

Even when he accompanied Sonia during campaigning, Rahul preferred to stay in the background. At a rally in Andhra Pradesh, unlike Priyanka who would always stand beside Sonia, smiling, waving and acknowledging greetings, he stood behind his mother on the dais and hardly spoke. But the crowd which had spotted him wanted more of him, and he was persuaded to move to the front row and sit next to Sonia. Gauging the mood, Sonia too gently nudged him forward so that people could get a better look at him. Throughout the campaign, Rahul's presence remained understated. He kept a low profile and rarely spoke to the media. So much so, that at one point of time it was rumoured that he had a speech impediment. In 1999, it was evident that many within and outside the Party saw Priyanka as the natural heir. In early 1999, Congressmen even hoped to persuade Priyanka to contest from Amethi, Rae Bareli or Sultanpur. But she chose to campaign rather than contest.

Sonia won from both Amethi and Bellary and chose to retain the Amethi seat. Rahul and Priyanka attended her oath-taking ceremony in the Lok Sabha. The difference between their personalities was visible even when they arrived at Parliament. Rahul got out of his car and went straight in. Priyanka paused and smiled for the cameras.

***

Although Sonia had won the election from two constituencies, the Congress did not return to power. Instead, the elections which ended in early October 1999 saw the Congress face an embarrassing defeat. The results were decisively in favour of the BJP-led NDA. After three general elections in four years, the country finally had a coalition government that had a majority and would last a full five-year term. The Congress, under Sonia Gandhi, had to settle for the opposition benches in Parliament. The rebellion within the Congress early that year on the issue of Sonia's foreign origins had not helped the Party's performance in the election. During the CWC's meeting on 15 May that year, Sharad Pawar,

P.A. Sangma and Tariq Anwar, Sitaram Kesri's protégé, had openly rebelled against Sonia and demanded that the issue of her nationality be settled once and for all. Sonia, who had made India her home thirty years ago when she married Rajiv, was shocked, and so were Rahul and Priyanka. Both advised her to resign from the post of Congress president and together drafted her resignation letter. The three rebels, meanwhile, broke away from the Congress to set up the Nationalist Congress Party. Senior Congress leaders and party workers got down to pacifying Sonia and coaxing her to take back her resignation. On one occasion, party supporters surrounded Rahul when he returned home late in the evening and begged him to urge his mother to change her mind. The three—Sonia, Rahul and Priyanka—finally decided to put the past behind them and focus on the elections.

In 1999, people had already started speculating about the fifth generation of the Nehru–Gandhi clan entering politics. Five years later, when the country faced another general election, the question of which one of the two Gandhi siblings would contest was again asked. It was expected, both by the Party and the media, that the dynasty would continue. In a television interview in 1998, Sonia had said, 'Both my children are extremely interested in politics, but they are not interested at the moment to be active in politics.' Of Rahul, she said, 'When my son is not here, and when we talk on the phone, most of the questions are related to what is happening in politics.' Priyanka, too, she added was very 'interested in politics'. This wasn't the first time the family had been asked about the possibility of Rahul and Priyanka entering politics. When he was prime minister, Rajiv had been asked which one of the two would be more suitable for politics and he had replied, 'It's difficult to say who is more suitable for politics. I wouldn't have said I was suited for politics but here I am.' He also said, 'Like all brothers and sisters, they have a lot in common and yet there are differences . . . Priyanka is strong-willed. Rahul is a much more outgoing, sporting type of person, and much more sensitive, perhaps.'

By 2004, Congressmen had a faint inkling that Sonia was keener on Rahul's donning the mantle. Priyanka, who had married Delhi businessman Robert Vadra on 18 February 1997, was now a mother. 'Sonia felt politics would take up too much of her time and did not want her family to be neglected. Her traditional Catholic upbringing has taught her to put the family first,' said a Congressman. 'The three of them take every important decision after discussing it among themselves.

Together, they decided that Priyanka should stay in the background and focus on her family while Rahul carries forward the Nehru–Gandhi legacy.' So, while across the political circles, the air was thick with speculation about Priyanka's entry into politics, none of this was reflected in her house: 35, Lodhi Estate. It was the house of a woman who took pride in being a good wife and a loving mother. A woman who, in her own words, often baked cupcakes for her children and helped them with their homework and wanted 'to lead a normal life'. In later years, she would often be seen at Delhi's Lodi Gardens, accompanying her children to karate lessons. At those times, she kept her distance from the media, politely telling those who approached her that this was her private life and she would like to keep it that way. Her security guards, though always around, would stay concealed behind the bushes and trees in the garden while the children went about their lessons. But there was another dimension to her life. Priyanka, the homemaker, was also Congress's most charismatic campaigner. Despite the distinctly domestic mood in her house and the shell she went into when she was involved in activities concerning her children, many within the Party hoped that, this time around, she would cross the thin line that separated the campaigner from the candidate.

A similar hope revolved around Rahul who had moved back to India in 2002 and had dropped everything to campaign for his mother and the Congress. He had started taking active interest in politics and was seen more frequently with his mother at public events. Several newspapers, magazines and television channels carried out polls to weigh how Congress's fortunes would change if Priyanka and Rahul campaigned or, better still, contested. Every poll threw up similar results. Voters felt Priyanka's and Rahul's entry into politics would improve the Congress's chances. The majority seemed to agree that it was time Priyanka and Rahul entered active politics. And finally, most of them felt that Priyanka—and not Rahul—was the natural inheritor of the Nehru–Gandhi legacy. Opinions hadn't changed since 1984 when India had first noticed Priyanka Gandhi during her grandmother Indira's funeral. Twenty years later, a TV-journalist-turned-columnist went to the extent of writing that Priyanka has it and Rahul doesn't.

The siblings, meanwhile, continued to dodge the question which now followed them everywhere. They encountered it again when they visited Amethi and Rae Bareli in early 2004 to meet with party workers and interact with the people. Again, Priyanka did most of the talking while Rahul remained an observer. She spoke to party workers, office bearers, and the men and women of the two constituencies. He preferred to chat with the children. The cameras followed them both, but Rahul tried to keep a distance between him and the lens. Priyanka, instead, flashed her infectious smile as she went about her work. For many years, the people of Amethi hoped Priyanka would stand for elections. Election after election, the popular slogan in Amethi had been, 'Amethi ka danka, bitiya Priyanka (The clarion call from Amethi is for our daughter Priyanka to contest elections).'

'Rahul Gandhi left the country during Rajivji's time and largely remained abroad from 1987 onwards. It was his sister who would visit Amethi and look after the constituency along with the Congress president or in her absence,' recalled a Congress leader from Amethi. 'Then in 2003, as we started preparations for the next year's Lok Sabha elections, instructions came from the top for an office be set up in Rae Bareli. Soon, we started operating from Pandey Kothi [Sonia Gandhi's current office in her constituency]. It was clearly Priyanka who was to contest from either of the two constituencies,' he added.

It was going to be a difficult election. The Congress realized that. Opinion polls and newspaper columns were flooded with grim predictions for the Party. The

NDA government thought it had done fairly well in the five years that it had been in power and was confident of winning the election on issues of governance and development. The Vajpayee government launched a multi-crore 'feel good' campaign which it called 'India Shining'. It sold the idea of a new India, a nation to be reckoned with, an India with a global presence. The Congress struggled to come up with a counter-plan. To some extent, India was shining, but it was shining for only a select few. To the vast majority of Indians, not even a faint glimmer was visible. The Congress decided to tap this vast majority. The Party's campaign managers, led by Jairam Ramesh, came up with the slogan, '*Congress ka haath, garib ke saath* (The hand of the Congress is with the poor).' The 'hand' here was the symbol of the party. The slogan was reminiscent of Indira's *garibi hatao* (eradicate poverty) call but, somehow, it didn't seem to click. Brainstorming sessions, with Rahul actively participating, followed. He and Jairam convinced the Party to replace the word *garib* (poor) with *aam aadmi* (the common man). The country was no longer dealing only with poverty which had been the single biggest challenge in the years after Independence. The economy had opened up and people had dreams of a better life. The slogan, it was felt, should connect with the common man and his aspirations, and at the same time question NDA's claim that India was shining. At Rahul's behest, the *aam aadmi*, replaced the Congress's garib. And now, the Congress had its slogan: '*Congress ka haath, aam aadmi ke saath* (The hand of the Congress is with the common man).' The question that the Congress posed at NDA's India Shining campaign was simple: '*Aam aadmi ko kya mila?* (What did the common man get out of India Shining?)' The question remained central to Rahul Gandhi's politics in the years to follow. In 2009, while targeting NDA's India Shining campaign, he said:

In 2004, they gave you a slogan, 'India Shining'. And we gave you a slogan 'government of common man'. 'India Shining' was in English and half of the population in India could not understand it . . . They did not go to the houses of the poor, the farmers, the Dalit and other weaker sections. They just went to the houses of the rich. We made just one promise— that we will work for the '*aam aadmi*', farmers of Punjab, *mazdoor* [labourers], Dalit and it will be their government.

In April 2004, *Outlook* quoted the Party strategist Jairam Ramesh saying that Rahul had taken personal interest in the Congress's election manifesto. He had wanted it 'sleekly packaged, reader-friendly, pictorial and full of action plans instead of promises'. Completely involved with the campaigning, he advised Sonia to concentrate on *jan sampark* (mass contact) programmes rather than focus her energy on holding rallies, a norm during election campaigns, where it is not unusual for the crowd to be paid to come to the venue. He also turned his attention to the Congress website and wanted it to reflect the Party's plans and achievements. By now, many in the Congress had started to feel that even though Rahul did not have the kind of political exposure his younger sister did, he was better informed, extremely well-read and far-sighted. But several others were of the opinion that Priyanka knew the pulse of both the party worker and the voter much better than Rahul. And that she was more charismatic. They felt she had the ability to reach out to people and touch hearts, unlike Rahul who was not as spontaneous. 'She knows where to stop the convoy and talk to the people,' said a family associate. 'She remembers people's names and their problems. When she sees a familiar face in the crowd, she makes it a point to address that person by name. And what an impression that leaves!' One of Priyanka's loyalists also brings out a monthly magazine called the *World of Priyanka*. In fact, there are about half a dozen such cheaply brought out periodicals in Amethi and Rae Bareli with no fixed periodicity, eulogizing the Gandhi family.

The suspense finally ended on 5 April 2004 when Rahul Gandhi filed his nomination papers for the Amethi constituency in Sultanpur. Sonia stood to his right. Priyanka stood behind him, her right arm stretched over his shoulder, holding the nomination papers in place for him. Rahul would contest the election. Priyanka would continue to campaign. With Rahul contesting from Amethi, Sonia shifted her constituency to Rae Bareli, a relatively tougher seat compared to Amethi. The writing was on the wall. Rahul was given a constituency which had been a Congress stronghold for decades; his victory was certain. The launch pad, the Congress knew, had to be firm; there was no way the Party could afford to have him lose his first election. Priyanka managed the campaign for both her mother and her brother. In March 2004, before he filed his nomination papers, Rahul visited Amethi with Priyanka who introduced him to the party workers there, saying, 'He will look after you now.'

The BJP started getting the jitters. It was easy to target Sonia, what with her shaky Hindi, limited political experience and, most importantly, foreign origin. But with Rahul and Priyanka both appearing on the scene, the battle strategy had to be redrawn. Both had charisma. Both were young and drew crowds wherever they went. And the 'foreign origin' tag did not apply to them. The BJP's India Shining campaign now began to totter. The 1999 slogans that had attacked Sonia's foreign origins; fresh slogans against dynastic politics; and the almost-forgotten issue of the Bofors gun case—everything in the BJP's arsenal was pulled out to target the Gandhi troika. The NDA manifesto which was released in early April also promised a law that would bar people of foreign origin from holding 'important offices of the Indian state'. Armed with these defences, the BJP was almost sure of riding to victory on what Deputy Prime Minister L.K. Advani described as the 'feel good factor'.

Political analysts, too, did not see much hope for the Congress in this election. They couldn't have been more off the mark. A poll conducted by CVoter for Star TV in Uttar Pradesh found that most voters believed that, in the long run, the Congress would benefit from having Rahul in the Party. But these predictions were restricted to the state of Uttar Pradesh. The 2004 election results stumped not just the political pandits, it also caught the Congress by surprise. The mandate was clearly in its favour. The Party was able to cobble together a majority government, the UPA, without much effort.

'The only one who had the numbers exact was my brother,' Priyanka told *Outlook* in the run-up to the next election. 'All the rest of us thought we were not going to do well,' she said. She also said that her brother was 'far more astute politically' than her. 'His understanding of social and economic issues is way above mine,' Priyanka said. Having taken the backseat herself, she has been among Rahul's biggest advocates and has often projected her brother as a forward-thinking politician. In an NDTV interview in 2009, she said:

> One thing that I admire about my brother is that he has this ability to be focussed on what he wants to do ... Remember the UP election, where he was berated and everything was piled on to him? But he just went ahead with what he thought was right. The other thing that I think is great about him as a politician is that he doesn't have this thing that he absolutely has to succeed every time. And, he's very good with things in which, perhaps, in the short term, he won't succeed but he can see that there is a long-term success. He will work through that short-term failure.

Priyanka also dismissed what people had been saying for years, that it was she and not Rahul who had Indira's political acumen. Rahul, she said, was the one in the family who had taken after Indira.

> She [Indira] taught him and spent a lot of time with him, talking to him. I think Rahul has imbibed a lot of that. His thinking is in many ways a lot like my father's because he is a visionary like that. He is an institution-builder like my father was but it's a good mix. His understanding of politics is really very good, much better than he is given credit for and that, I think, comes from my grandmother.

While campaigning for him that year, when she once again dismissed the question of her contesting an election, one reporter asked her if that meant she would never enter politics. Priyanka replied that life and experience had taught her never to say never. Was that a sign of things to come in the near future? With the Nehru–Gandhi family, that possibility cannot be ruled out. After a series of crises hit the UPA government in 2011, the murmurs of Priyanka contesting the next general election grew louder.

Election 2004, meanwhile, clearly established Rahul's presence in Indian politics. It also saw Sonia emerge as a seasoned politician with an uncanny ability to feel the pulse of the country and stump the Opposition. Having won the election, Sonia Gandhi, as Congress president, had every right to become prime minister of the country. It also seemed obvious that she would. But Sonia chose otherwise. On 18 May 2004, she made a brief speech declining the post. She said the post of prime minister 'is not my aim. I was always certain that if ever I found myself in the position that I am [in] today, I would follow my own inner voice. Today, that voice tells me I must humbly decline this post.' As stunned Congressmen tried to understand the import of her words, Sonia added, 'I appeal to you to understand the force of my conviction. I request you to accept my decision and recognize that I will not reverse it.'

The gesture won her acclaim across the world. The woman who could have been leader of the world's largest and most dynamic democracy had just given it up. It was a political masterstroke. Sonia continued to head the Party but handed over the prime-ministership to Dr Manmohan Singh, who had been the finance minister in the Narasimha Rao government and was seen within the Party as an intelligent, apolitical person, besides being an eminent economist. With that one move, Sonia won a million hearts and silenced her detractors who had called her a power-hungry foreigner. On 22 May 2004, Manmohan Singh was sworn in as prime minister of India. Sonia continued to hold the post of Congress president. Neither Rahul nor Priyanka had been in favour of Sonia's becoming prime minister. Rahul was convinced that turning down the prime minister's post was the right thing to do. It would be seen as an act of renunciation and trump her critics in the Opposition. For Priyanka, it was a big relief. Priyanka recalled how she had 'one moment of complete terror' when she saw senior leaders surrounding Sonia in her office asking her to become prime minister. She said she burst out crying and had run to Rahul.

Two years later, Sonia would find herself at the crossroads again. This time, the controversy whether she held an 'office of profit' as chairperson of the National Advisory Council (NAC) threatened to sully her image. She announced her resignation at a press conference at 10 Janpath with a resolute-looking Rahul standing to her left. He looked like a determined soldier with his hands clasped behind his back. Priyanka watched from behind a half-open door, barely visible through the curtains. The moment captured the political roles the three had defined for themselves.

Sonia's decision to resign had found strong support in Rahul. He had felt that it would be appropriate for her to step down and go back to the masses. India values the spirit of sacrifice. That had become clear in 2004 when

Sonia shunned the prime minister's post. The latest controversy now threatened to weaken the gains of 2004. By stepping down, Sonia would again consolidate her image as an upright person who would not compromise on values for the sake of power. Rahul felt a win from Rae Bareli would be a befitting reply to the opposition—and it was. Sonia won with an even bigger margin than she had in 2004. All other candidates had to forfeit their deposits. Rahul played the manager's role in this election, holding over a dozen public meetings in a single day and staying in Rae Bareli for about three weeks. Confident of Rahul's work, Sonia only visited the constituency at the tail end of the campaign. Her victory was ascribed to Rahul's efforts even by the CWC. Priyanka's role remained limited to a few days of campaigning and being Sonia's polling agent. On the day of the polling and, later, when the results came out, the focus of the media's questions to her had shifted from 'When will you contest?' to 'When will Rahul be given a bigger role?'

The Shaping of the Personality

In the summer of 2008, Om Prakash Bhardwaj—India's top-notch boxing coach who had been honoured with the Dronacharya Award—received an unexpected call from the Sports Authority of India. He was told that someone from 10 Janpath would get in touch with him. Some time later, P. Madhavan, who had been on the personal staff of the Nehru–Gandhi family for over two decades, called with an unusual request: Rahul Gandhi wanted to learn boxing. Would Bhardwaj agree to teach him?

'I was surprised,' said Bhardwaj, who was nearing seventy then. 'Rahul couldn't have been planning to enter the boxing ring, of this I was sure. Perhaps he wanted lessons in self-defence, I thought.' Not wanting to let the opportunity pass, Bhardwaj promptly agreed. As for fees, all he wanted was to be picked from and dropped back at his house. The classes were to take place at 12 Tughlaq Lane where Rahul lived.

India was less than a year away from the next parliamentary elections. The UPA government, led by the Congress, had been in power for four years. The next test was nearing. Politicians in the country had slipped into election gear. Rahul did, too, with boxing lessons from Bhardwaj. The world of politics isn't very different from the boxing arena. The right moves made at the right time can turn the game around. Underestimating one's opponent can cost dearly. It is important to get into the mind of the rival and be prepared to strike and to defend simultaneously. Boxing and politics both call for patience, speed, timing and stamina.

Rahul learnt his lesson well. In the Lok Sabha elections that followed in 2009, he retained his Amethi seat by defeating his nearest rival, Asheesh Shukla of the ruling Bahujan Samaj Party, by over 3.7 lakh votes. Not only this, the Congress which had, for over two decades, been reduced to a marginal player in Uttar Pradesh, struck hard and re-emerged as a party to watch out for. Rahul had decided to break into the formidable Mayawati's territory and the Party won twenty-one of the eighty Lok Sabha seats. Before the elections, an energetic RG, as he's called within the Party, also spoke at 125 rallies, travelling more than 80,000 kilometres across India in a span of just six weeks—his numbers were higher than those of any other politician in that election. The physical endurance that he had built up during the boxing lessons came in useful.

Bhardwaj, who had decided to observe Rahul very closely not just as a student but as a man who was being touted as the future prime minister of India, said, 'He was always ready for more. If I told him to run one round of the lawn to warm up, he would run three.'

The boxing sessions were held three days a week on the lawns of 12 Tughlaq Lane. At times, Priyanka and her children would also come to watch Rahul train. Sonia, too, would sometimes sit and watch. 'One day, Priyanka asked me to teach her as well,' said Bhardwaj. He explained some boxing moves to the younger and equally athletic Gandhi sibling and was quite taken aback by the punch she threw: 'It was a beautiful punch, totally unexpected from someone trying her hand at boxing for the first time.'

The scene that summer wasn't very different from the way it used to be when, as children, Rahul and Priyanka were forced to take private lessons at home due to security reasons after Indira was assassinated.

***

The day Indira was shot, Rajiv Gandhi was on an election tour in West Bengal. When he flew back to Delhi that day, the road from the airport to AIIMS was lined with security 'unprecedented in the history of the country', as a *Time* magazine report noted. Sharpshooters were positioned by the road on either side. Satwant Singh, one of Indira's two assassins who survived the counterattack by his colleagues, told his interrogators that Rajiv, too, was a target of those who had planned the assassination. As Rajiv settled down in his new job as prime minister succeeding his mother, the task of protecting him and his family was taken away from the Intelligence Bureau and the Delhi police and entrusted to the newly raised Special Protection Group (SPG).

After Operation Blue Star, Indira had been advised against having Sikh bodyguards around her. All Sikh officers posted at 1 Safdarjung Road had been quietly withdrawn. But Indira was not happy with the decision. She said she could not be called a secular prime minister if she took such a step. On her insistence, the Sikh security guards were redeployed at her residence, but with riders. Rameshwar Nath Kao, Indira's security adviser and the first chief of the Research and Analysis Wing (R&AW), gave strict instructions that no Sikh bodyguard was to be posted near her alone, writes B. Raman, former head of R&AW's counterterrorism division, in his book, *The Kaoboys of R&AW: Down Memory Lane*. Every Sikh security guard deployed close to her would be accompanied by a non-Sikh officer. Under no circumstances would two Sikh officers be deployed together. Despite the stringent security measures, Satwant Singh and Beant Singh succeeded in manipulating the roster. On the morning of 31 October 1984, the two were positioned not far from each other and in close proximity to the prime minister at her residence. Kao was in Beijing that day. That's where he received the news of Indira's assassination. He immediately flew back to Delhi on a special plane arranged by the Chinese government, and later resigned from his post.

Indira's death was followed by anti-Sikh violence of the worst kind in New Delhi and one that the government machinery did little to contain. At best, it looked the other way. Nearly 3,000 Sikhs were killed in the violence. There was violence in other parts of the country, too, but it was the most widespread and prolonged in the national capital. Rajiv was sworn in as prime minister the same evening. Indira had thought of her Sikh bodyguards being taken off duty as a non-secular act and had ordered them right back; Rajiv, on the other hand, seemed to have reacted more out of a sense of personal loss rather than as prime minister of the nation when he remarked on the violence saying, 'When a big tree falls, the earth shakes.' His remark did little to assuage the feelings of the Sikhs first shaken by Operation Blue Star in June 1984 and then by the young prime minister's inaction against the rioters. These decisions only increased the family's own security concerns.

With intelligence reports confirming that Rajiv and his family were on the hit list, their security became an issue of immediate concern. So far, the Intelligence Bureau had coordinated and supervised all security matters related to the prime minister. But providing physical security was the responsibility of the police. There was no exclusive, dedicated agency to look after the security of the prime minister of India. On 8 April 1985, the SPG came into being to fill the gap. Its task was to ensure the protection of the prime minister's family—Sonia, Rahul and Priyanka—as well as of Rajiv Gandhi. A tight security ring was formed around them, cutting them off from the outside world.

The Gandhis also moved from 1 Safdarjung Road to 7 Race Course Road, which has remained the official residence of the prime minister of India ever since. Rajiv was the first prime minister to occupy this address. With security guards spread across the premises, the house practically became a prison for Rajiv's family. 'The only space outside our four walls where we could step without a cordon of security was our garden,' wrote Sonia in her book, *Rajiv*. After Indira was killed, Sonia feared that her family would also meet the same fate that had befallen Bangladesh President, Sheikh Mujibur Rahman, and his family. Rahman was assassinated in August 1975 in a bloody military coup along with his wife, three sons (one of whom was barely ten), two daughters-in-law, his brother, a nephew and eighteen other people.

It was in this atmosphere of high security—heightened by Indira's fear for the safety of her family and later compounded by her killing—that Rahul spent his childhood. The security cover brought with it several restrictions, including homeschooling. The day Indira was killed was the last day that Rahul and Priyanka went to school. For the next five years the children were taught at home. Being an 'outgoing, sporting type of person', in Rajiv's words, Rahul found ways to pursue his interest in sports. He went swimming, cycling and scuba-diving, and played squash. Like his father, Rahul trained at a shooting range in the Aravalli ranges near Delhi, and also learnt to fly.

His interest in sports later earned him a seat in the much sought-after St. Stephen's College in Delhi in 1989. Rahul could not make it into the college on the basis of his academic score but was, instead, admitted under the sports quota for his skill in pistol shooting. He had enrolled for an honours degree in history. He would come to college accompanied by security guards and was mostly a backbencher in class. Though he had been quite a sport during the ragging session, he seldom spoke during the rest of his time in college. After one year and three months, he dropped out of St. Stephen's. Like everybody else, the principal of the college, Dr Anil Wilson, could only speculate about the reason for Rahul's leaving the course midway. He had found Rahul to be a down-to-earth person who had no airs about being a member of the Gandhi family. He felt that Rahul was embarrassed by the tight security that followed him everywhere and that was probably the reason he abandoned the course.

St. Stephen's was happy to have had the young Gandhi among its students, even if only briefly. But a remark that Rahul made eighteen years later while discussing the state of education in the country left many Stephanians fuming. In October 2008, while addressing students at a university in Srinagar, Rahul said, 'When I was studying at St. Stephen's College, asking a question was not [perceived to be] good in our class. You were looked down upon if you asked too many questions.' Rahul was trying to highlight the weaknesses in the Indian higher education system, where he said that completing the syllabus takes precedence over liberal discussion. But the remark upset the college faculty, students and alumni.

Principal Dr Valson Thampu dismissed the criticism saying, 'What Mr Gandhi said is his personal experience and there's no reason to believe otherwise. It can certainly not be correct to make such a generalization about the overall academic environment at the college.' But he also graciously added that Rahul might have felt so because he was part of the largest class. 'History has nearly sixty students in every class,' Thampu said, alluding to the fact that the large number could have reduced personal interaction between the teachers and the students.

However, not every member of the faculty took as kindly to the statement. One teacher said that the college had nearly thirty-six clubs and forums, apart from informal discussion groups which were open to students from across all courses, but Rahul had hardly participated in any of these. Making concessions for the young Gandhi, Thampu said security issues might have restricted his participation in these college activities.

Soon after leaving St. Stephen's College, Rahul headed for the United States and joined Harvard University as a student of economics. He was twenty years old. He had spent barely a year at Harvard when his father was assassinated. The tragedy took its toll on Rahul's education. Again, security concerns were cited as the reason for Rahul's leaving Harvard and moving to Rollins College, a private institute of liberal arts in Winter Park, Florida. The suburban city, which was initially created by rich industrialists as a resort destination, offered the ideal atmosphere to the young man whose life had until now been spent under the vigil of security guards. This time, Rahul completed the course for which he had enrolled and, in 1994, graduated with a degree in international relations, one of the six majors taught at the college.

Rahul went on to attend Trinity College at Cambridge. His great-grandfather, Jawaharlal Nehru, had also studied at the same college from 1907 to 1910 and earned a degree in law. Rajiv, too, had studied mechanical engineering at Trinity. Rahul opted for an MPhil in development studies which he completed in 1995. But in April 2009, soon after he filed his nomination papers from the Amethi constituency in Uttar Pradesh, his academic qualifications were questioned. A newspaper carried a report saying that Rahul had registered for the MPhil course in 2004–05 and not 1994–95, as claimed in his nomination papers. The news report also said that it wasn't certain whether Rahul had completed the course.

The Congress was furious. The news report, published before the 2009 Lok Sabha elections, was damning and neither Rahul nor the Party was willing to let the matter pass. A legal notice, drafted by Congress spokesperson and Supreme Court lawyer Abhishek Manu Singhvi, was served on the newspaper. It read, 'Deeply distressed by your wild allegations, sly insinuations and self-serving innuendos, all premised on complete falsehoods and steeped in malice, a legal notice is being issued.' Attached to the notice was a copy of a letter from Dame Alison Fettes Richard, vice chancellor of the University of Cambridge. The letter said that Rahul had been a student of Trinity College from October 1994 to July 1995 and had received an MPhil in development studies in 1995. Professor Richard wrote, 'It is extremely unfortunate that a controversy has arisen regarding your degree and we would like to set the controversy at rest immediately.' She added that Rahul's conduct at the university was 'exemplary and he remained a good student throughout'.

Rahul did not return to India immediately after passing out of Trinity College. Instead, he took up a job in London with the Monitor Group, a global management and strategy consultancy firm co-founded by Michael Eugene Porter, a professor at Harvard Business School, and considered to be a leading authority on brand strategy. Rahul worked there for three years, but under an assumed name. His colleagues had little idea that they had the grandson of Indira in their midst. Speaking of the need for privacy that had always eluded him, Rahul said, 'After studies in the US, I risked my life to do away with my guards to lead a regular life in England.' His father had felt the same need to get away. After Rajiv became prime minister, when time for himself and his family became a luxury and his passion for flying got pushed back by the momentum of politics, he said, 'I sometimes get into the cockpit, all alone, and close the door. Even if I cannot fly, at least I can temporarily shut myself off from the outside world.'

While Rahul tried to lead a regular life in England, back in India, his mother Sonia was getting deeply involved in politics. Having agreed to enter politics in 1997, she was now leading the Congress from the front. Through it all, Priyanka stood by her side, becoming her pillar of support. Within the Congress, the clamour for Priyanka to join the Party was growing. Rahul had been away from the country for over ten years now. But the political atmosphere back home indicated that it was time to return. And he did, in 2002.

India was witnessing a boom in the outsourcing industry. Western multinational corporations were turning to India to get jobs done faster and more cheaply. Rahul set up an engineering and technology outsourcing firm, Backops Services Private Ltd, in the country's commercial nerve centre, Mumbai. The BPO venture employed just eight people and, according to its application to the Registrar of Companies, its business objectives included providing advisory support to domestic and international clients; acting as a consultant and adviser in the field of information technology; and offering web solutions. Rahul was one of its directors, along with family friend Manoj Muttu. The other two directors—Anil Thakur, the son of Congress leader and former Union minister Rameshwar Thakur, and Delhi resident Ranvir Sinha—resigned in March 2006, citing 'personal reasons'. According to his affidavit to the Election Commission of India before the 2004 general elections, Rahul held 83 per cent of the shares in Backops Services Private Ltd. The company's balance sheet indicated that it was a modest business venture.

Soon after Rahul entered politics in 2004, his company advertised that it was looking for a CEO. 'We are searching for a CEO, though I hold periodic meetings with the employees and look at the larger issues,' Rahul told the *Business Standard* in June 2004. At that time, the company had three overseas clients and by Rahul's admission, it did not have any revenues in the first year of operation. In 2009, shortly before the Lok Sabha elections, Rahul opted out of this business venture. According to Congressmen, the demands of politics left him with little time to run the business.

There were breaks in Rahul's career trajectory as there had been in his education. But the one thing that remained consistent was Rahul's obsession with physical fitness and adventure sports. No matter how packed the day, he would find time to exercise. The year Rahul did a crash course in boxing, he also took lessons in paragliding.

Putting his management training to use, he took along his team of seven to eight people from Amethi to Nirvana Adventures, a flying club at Kamshet in Maharashtra. The three-day long paragliding course that lasted from 28 to 30 January 2008, also served as a team-building exercise. Situated in the Western Ghats, 85 kilometres from Pune, Kamshet was not the usual setting where a politician and his party workers would get together to discuss work.

But, with Rahul's track record of not doing what you would expect politicians to do, it wasn't that unusual. In the midst of sunflower fields, quiet lakes and hills dotted with ancient Buddhist cave temples, the Amethi team spent the mornings taking paragliding lessons and the evenings brainstorming. Those who watched them at Kamshet said the discussions took place one-on-one. The hierarchy was visible only when the team addressed Rahul: they all called him Rahul *bhaiyya*.

Before Rahul and his men landed at Kamshet, his host Astrid Rao had been very apprehensive about the high-profile politician visiting her quiet hamlet. Astrid, who founded Nirvana Adventures along with her husband Sanjay Rao, was certain the visit would disturb the peace of the area. 'I was sure the area would be cordoned off by the tight security that would accompany Rahul,' she said. None of that happened. 'Without our mentioning it, Rahul ensured that nobody in uniform or with guns was seen in or around the guest house. Not once was our routine disrupted by his presence,' Astrid said.

It was like having any other guest. The first night, the Raos cooked lamb for their visitors. A buffet was laid. 'I was surprised to see Rahul offering plates to the others with him. He also made it a point to leave his plate in the kitchen himself,' said Astrid. The next day, mealtime found Rahul going up to the cook to ask him if there was any lamb left over from the previous night.

Coach Bhardwaj, too, described Rahul as a man with no airs. 'When I started training him, I addressed him as "Sir" or "Rahulji".' But two days into the training, Rahul made a request to his coach, 'Please don't call me "Sir". Call me Rahul, I'm your student.' On another occasion, Bhardwaj said he told Rahul that he wanted to have some water. 'There were attendants standing nearby, but instead of calling one of them, Rahul went running into the kitchen and got me a glass of water.' And after the lessons, Rahul would escort his teacher to the gate.

At the paragliding school in Kamshet, Rahul's first day was spent with flight trainer Sanjay Rao who gave him ground training. Actual flight lessons were carried out on the last two days. 'Rahul's performance was very good. He just picked up the glider and was off,' said Sanjay, rating Rahul among the top 10 per cent of his students. 'He is a very attentive listener which is why he learns fast.' Those who have observed him describe him as a man 'who always keeps his antennae up'. During the stay, Rahul also wanted to go for a swim in the nearby lake, but his security guards advised him against it. He heeded their advice. 'It was a pity, considering that he's a very athletic person and likes to jog upto 10 kilometres a day,' said Astrid.

As word got out that the young Gandhi was training at Kamshet, several local villagers turned up to meet him. Among them was an old farmer, a familiar face in the Kamshet area. The Raos introduced him to Rahul as 'Shelar *mama*'. The farmer did a big namaskar and then, with hands that shook with age, he poured Rahul tea in a dirty cup which he had brought along. Everybody flinched. 'But without hesitating for a second, Rahul took the cup from Shelar mama's hands, drank the tea and then asked for another cup,' said Astrid. That's another trait he has inherited from his father. While campaigning in the heat of Amethi, Rajiv would willingly, and gratefully, reach out for a glass of water or sherbet offered by women waiting at the doors of their ramshackle huts for the visiting leader.

The farmer from Kamshet, who is said to have been a pearl diver once, went on to tell an attentive Rahul one story after the other about his life and travels. Other elderly men also came to meet him. They would walk up to him with hands folded in a greeting and Rahul would promptly stand up. He wouldn't sit until they did. Those who know the young Gandhi say this is normal behaviour for him. Like his father and sister, Rahul is not comfortable being treated like a demi-god. He doesn't like people touching his feet or standing in attendance around him. He would rather sit on the floor with them.

He is also not a man to forget a promise. Astrid discovered this a month after Rahul and his team left Kamshet. When she had taken him on a tour of her garden, Rahul had told her that his mother was also fond of gardening. He said Sonia had a particular book to which she often referred, but he could not recall its title. He promised to send it to her after he got back to Delhi. A month later, Astrid received an unexpected parcel. It was the gardening book Rahul had talked about.

Rahul doesn't forget. Nor does he forgive. A group of journalists learnt this the hard way. On 22 January 2009, the NSUI filed a police complaint at Rahul's behest after the notes made for his speech and presentation went missing from the venue of a convention during the lunch break. The incident took place at the Constitution Club in Delhi where a party workshop was being held. It was suspected that the papers were picked up by members of a TV crew who had entered the hall when all the others had gone for lunch. About twenty-five journalists were present at the venue. NSUI chief Hibi Eden filed a complaint at the Parliament Street police station. It is said the step was taken after Rahul insisted that the matter be reported to the police. Journalists will often go the extra mile for more information but, to him, picking up someone's papers to get information that had not been shared constituted theft. For two days, the police called and questioned three television journalists from different channels over Rahul's missing papers. Though members of Rahul's team also tried to reason with him that, at the end of the day, the papers only pertained to a presentation that he was making and did not contain any secrets, he insisted on taking the journalists to task.

Within the Party, too, he is known to frown upon mistakes. 'He will not suffer fools,' Priyanka said in a TV interview in 2009 during the Lok Sabha elections. In December 2009, the Uttar Pradesh Congress Committee chief Rita Bahuguna Joshi created a flutter when she said that Rahul had forced his helicopter to land in conditions of zero visibility on an airstrip in UP's Sitapur district. Rahul was on a two-day visit to UP to add steam to the Youth Congress membership drive. 'He had promised to meet backward class people in Sitapur,' said Joshi. 'Rahulji is so deeply committed about keeping his promise that, despite the delay, he persuaded the pilot to land in total darkness and zero-visibility conditions, without paying any heed to the risk to his own life,' she announced.

Joshi's intention was to praise Rahul and perhaps win brownie points from a leader who projects himself as a representative of the poor and the backward. But the move boomeranged. Such a declaration coming barely three months after Andhra Pradesh Chief Minister Y.S. Rajasekhara Reddy had died in a helicopter crash in the Nallamala forests of Andhra Pradesh was not the kind of controversy the Congress wanted. An inquiry committee was already looking into what had caused the crash that cost the Party a popular chief minister. As an embarrassed Congress rushed to carry out damage control, Rahul told the media, 'I am a pilot myself and am well aware of the dangers of landing in poor visibility. I am absolutely the last person to even suggest a thing like that.' With a sheepish Joshi standing behind him, he said, 'The UP Congress chief is neither a pilot nor a weather expert. She does not know.'

***

On 19 June 2011, Rahul Gandhi turned forty-one. Though he lives the busy life of a politician, he pursues his hobbies and, like his parents, looks for ways to lead an ordinary life. When her husband was still a pilot and Indira the prime minister, Sonia was often spotted buying vegetables in Delhi's Khan Market. She loved to cook. Priyanka, too, likes to do her grocery shopping in the same market. Ranked among the world's most expensive retail high streets, Khan Market is also Rahul's favourite hangout in Delhi. He can be spotted having coffee at Barista or scanning through books in the shops on the outer side of the market. He also loves to spend time with his niece, Miraya, and nephew, Raihan. 'It's evident that he dotes on Priyanka's children,' said his hosts at Kamshet. During the paragliding trip, he was always talking about them and Priyanka. 'He often said, "Priyanka must come to this place, but she is lazy,"' said Astrid.

If a quiet evening out appeals to Rahul, so does life on the fast track. An official who worked closely with Manmohan Singh in the first term of the UPA government, said that Rahul would quietly fly to Singapore during the Grand Prix season, a high-octane affair when the city streets turn into a Formula One racing track. The days are packed with music concerts and parties.

An avid biker, Rahul also enjoys go-karting with his group of close friends. In April 2011, during a World Cup cricket match in Mumbai, Rahul landed at the New Yorker restaurant on Chowpatty beach around 1.30 in the afternoon for a meal of pizza, pasta and Mexican tostada salad. He chatted with the waiter and firmly turned down the manager's request to let the meal be on the house. Rahul and his friends then split the bill of Rs 2,233.

To this day, at the age of forty-one, Rahul Gandhi remains a bachelor. Every now and then, there is speculation about his marriage or the women in his life. One rare occasion on which he spoke openly about it was in 2004, soon after filing his nomination papers for the Amethi constituency. In an interview to Vrinda Gopinath of the *Indian Express*, he said, 'My girlfriend's name is Veronique not Juanita. She is Spanish and not Venezuelan or Colombian. She is an architect, not a waitress, though I wouldn't have had a problem with that. She is also my best friend.' Rahul, who had met Veronique when he was at university in England, also said he wasn't sure when he would settle down.

In the years since his first election victory, Rahul and the people around him have made no reference to his 'best friend', Veronique. For the Party which still faces barbs from the Opposition on grounds of Sonia's Italian roots, even though she made this country her home more than forty years ago, this is a sensitive subject.

Between Two Plenaries:
The Rise of Rahul Gandhi

Five years is a reasonably long time in politics. It is—if all goes well for the incumbent government—the gap between two general elections. Since Lok Sabhas have gone back to lasting their full terms in the past decade or so, a new member of the Lok Sabha would, in five years, go from being a newbie to a second-term MP if he or she is re-elected. And some would hope to play a slightly bigger role than they did the last time around. But, with Rahul Gandhi being no ordinary MP, it was only to be expected that in the five years that lapsed between the Congress's 82nd plenary session at

Hyderabad in January 2006 and the one in December 2010 held in Delhi to mark the completion of 125 years of the Party, his growth trajectory would be steeper than that of any other young politician. The gap between the two plenaries established him as one of the most powerful general secretaries of the Indian National Congress ever. It could probably also go down as one of the most significant five-year periods in Rahul's political journey. The proceedings of the 2010 plenary established that beyond doubt.

The Hyderabad session opened on 21 January 2006, at the GMC Balayogi Stadium at Gachibowli which had been decked up for the event. By the second week of January, the entire city of Hyderabad looked like the venue for the grand old party's plenary. The area around the stadium was named Rajiv Nagar, temporarily, after former Congress prime minister Rajiv Gandhi. It is common practice among political parties to name the venues of their plenaries and party congresses after their leaders. The party documents and resolutions carry these names, bearing witness to the Party's attempts to immortalize their leaders. It is at these plenaries which take place every few years that the existing leadership meets to assess the course charted by the Party, and plans for the future.

At the beginning of the Hyderabad plenary, it seemed as if the course for the future would be decided by the workers instead of by the leadership. The demand for a greater role for Rahul had reached a crescendo. On the eve of the plenary, Jitin Prasada, the young, first-time MP from Shahjahanpur (and son of a former Congress leader and vice-president Jitendra Prasada) had written to the Uttar Pradesh Congress Committee (UPCC) president Salman Khurshid that the youth of UP wanted the Amethi MP to take up a bigger role. Prasada's letter said that he was writing on behalf of the youth of the state whose aspiration was to see Rahul play the leader in Congress affairs. He said he had travelled widely in UP since the 2004 Lok Sabha polls and come back with this feedback. Prasada's letter obviously found its way to the press. Asked about the letter, he and Khurshid, or for that matter any other Congress leader, were only too eager to talk about the demand and stress the need for Rahul's inclusion in the Party's top brass.

Congressmen were shouting slogans asking for Rahul to be included in the Party's apex decision-making body, the CWC, and bestowing upon him a 'larger role'. Though the Congress, fresh after its surprise win of the mid-2004 general election, did not look like it needed any saving, *'Rahul lao, Congress bachao* (Bring Rahul Gandhi, save the

Congress).' slogans rent the air outside the precincts of the stadium. The AICC, the state committee workers and the mid-level netas jostled for airtime on channels, hoping to be seen as sloganeering to demand Rahul's promotion to the Party's higher echelons. Those higher in the hierarchy enthusiastically announced to the world, on television, that the time had come for gradually handing over the reins of the Congress. Party general secretary and former Madhya Pradesh chief minister Digvijaya Singh—who went on to become one of Rahul's closest advisers from the older generation of Congress leaders—told the media that it was only a matter of time before circumstances made it necessary for Rahul to shoulder greater responsibilities for the benefit of the Party and its political future. A news report in the *Times of India* on 22 January 2006 noted:

The country needs Reformist, Accomplished, Honest, Upcoming Leadership (RAHUL)' reads a billboard put up by the Youth Congress at a busy corner of the city. All India Congress Committee (AICC) general secretary Ambika Soni, along with central leaders Digvijaya Singh and Ashok Gehlot, has suggested that the young parliamentarian, elected from Amethi, play a more active role in the Party.

Soni said delegates might raise the demand for his nomination to the CWC.

A report in the *Tribune*, on the same day, said:

> AICC general secretary Ambika Soni is hot favourite for the TV cameras. Even as nothing much seems to be happening at the venue till evening, she is seen providing filler sound bites to the eager camera crews.
>
> The most sought-after comments, though repeated ad nauseam, are about Karnakata and Rahul's induction into the CWC. Ms Soni appeared particularly pleased to talk about Rahul. Couched in euphemisms, the purport of her message was that the party needs the young Gandhi badly, and it is up to Sonia to appoint him.

Rahul wasn't scheduled to speak at the plenary. But with the demand and the din for it peaking, he did make a stage appearance, almost coyly. On the first day of the proceedings, a chorus rose from the crowd demanding that Rahul speak. In order to pacify the crowds, he had to get up twice and promise to speak the next day. At that point, he was just the Amethi MP. He had largely confined himself to his constituency and neighbouring Rae Bareli. Despite the speculation, he did not join the Congress-led UPA government or accept a position in the Party organization.

When he spoke, politically, he made just one point: the Congress needed to revive itself in north India.

> In some states our organization is not working effectively. People give many reasons for this failure. They blame communal- and religion-based parties. I absolutely disagree with this assessment. My thinking on this issue is, we have failed only in those areas where we have stopped fighting for the voters and their problems.

He said this to Congressmen hiding behind the premise that Mandal-and-*mandir* politics had taken its toll on the Congress base. The last time the Congress had come to power on its own at the Centre was in 1991.

Contrast Rahul's opinion with Sonia Gandhi's address to the Party on 14 September 1998. Voted out of power in the 1996 general elections and then again in 1998, the Party had organized a brainstorming camp at Pachmarhi in Madhya Pradesh. The idea was to introspect and come up with ways to arrest the Congress decline. Compared to 1991, the Congress's vote share had gone down by more than 7 per cent in the 1996 elections. In 1998, it had dipped even further, by another 2 per cent or so. The panic-stricken Congress chose to go into a huddle over the losses at Pachmarhi. In her presidential remarks, Sonia said exactly what her son was to debunk as a false theory later at Hyderabad. As she listed out the reasons for the Party's decline, she said:

> Many of us thought that economic development and progress would roll back the spread of communal ideologies and put an end to the politics of hate. This has clearly not happened. The question we must ask ourselves is whether we have, in any way, diluted our commitment to the fight against communal forces. It would perhaps be tempting to say we have not. However, there is a general perception that we have at times compromised with our basic commitment to the secular ideal that forms the bedrock of our society. During our deliberations, we must all apply our minds to this vitally important question.

In the 1998 election, the BJP had secured only about 0.13 per cent fewer votes than the Congress, but it had bagged forty-one seats more than the latter—enough to cobble together a coalition and keep the Congress out of power. Among the Party's chief concerns was its decline in UP and Bihar, and caste-based politics was identified as the cause. Sonia said,

> Second, we must acknowledge that we have not successfully accommodated the aspirations of a whole new generation of Dalits, Adivasis and backward people, particularly in the northern parts of the country. Could this be one of the reasons for our decline in states like Uttar Pradesh and Bihar? Regrettably, we have not paid enough attention to the growth of such sentiments and feelings, and consequently have had to pay a heavy price. It is not enough to make promises. The Congress Party must ensure to this section of our people full and equal representation.

Years later, having debunked the Mandal–mandir theory as a reason for the Congress decline, Rahul added a footnote to his address with schoolboyish earnestness, 'Someone once asked me what my religion was. I thought about it and I answered that the Indian flag was my religion. And I promised myself after my father died that I would serve the people this flag represents.' Serve them he would, Rahul said, but,

> by taking up a job before I know what my people and workers feel and need, I will be doing a disservice both to my religion and to my party. It's time to learn and understand so that I can serve the people and the party better. I appreciate and I am grateful for your feelings and support. I assure you I will not let you down.

The speech and the plenary session at Hyderabad made it clear that the Gandhi scion wasn't yet ready to shoulder any responsibility in the government or the Party. It also established that he would steer the Party in a different direction despite not holding a formal position in the Congress organization.

Till the 2004 elections, Rahul's political pursuits had remained confined to visiting his parents' constituency, Amethi. Rajiv contested and won from Amethi four times between 1980 and 1991. After Sonia joined the Congress Party, she, too, contested from Amethi in 1999. Both children had often accompanied their parents on their visits to the constituency. It was familiar terrain for them but the public perception was that it would be Priyanka who would join politics. Then, in March 2004, came the announcement that Rahul would contest the elections from Amethi while Sonia would move to Rae Bareli.

Rahul sailed through the election without any difficulty not only because he was contesting from the safest seat for anyone from his family, but also because of the electorate's euphoria over ushering in a new generation of the Nehru–Gandhi clan into politics. A BBC report in March 2004, which followed the announcement of Rahul's candidature from Amethi, quoted locals from different castes and communities as saying that they would vote for him. 'Look at us here—a cross-section of voters of upper and lower castes, Hindus and a Muslim. We will all support them,' said a voter from among a group of local residents having tea at a shack. Living up to their expectations, Rahul toured Amethi (and Rae Bareli) extensively between the election victory of 2004 and the plenary of 2006. He learned to mingle with the locals of the two constituencies with which the Gandhi family shares a special bond.

Shortly after the plenary at Hyderabad, Sonia took everyone by surprise once again. She suddenly resigned from Parliament as well as from the chairpersonship of over a dozen bodies, including the NAC which had been formed to monitor the functioning of the government's policies. In 2004, she had turned down the offer to become prime minister and instead proposed Dr Manmohan Singh for the position. She had taken the decision after consultation with her two children. Rahul is said to have encouraged her to turn down the position and prove to the people that she was not in politics for personal gain. The move stumped the primary Opposition that had just lost the election—the National Democratic Alliance led by the BJP. The BJP had gone to great lengths to criticize the Congress, poking fun at it for not being able to find an Indian for the post of prime minister from among a billion people. Sushma Swaraj, who became leader of the Opposition in the 15th Lok Sabha, threatened to have her head tonsured if Sonia became prime minister. Sonia's refusal saved Sushma's tresses and cut short her histrionics.

A different set of actors—from Congress party workers threatening suicide to would-be cabinet ministers weeping on TV—took over the stage. But, once the din subsided, Manmohan Singh became prime minister of India. Sonia took charge of the NAC as chairperson soon after the United Progressive Alliance assumed power. The position accorded her a cabinet minister's rank. But, in the beginning of 2006, the Supreme Court disqualified Rajya Sabha MP Jaya Bachchan from membership of the upper house because, it ruled, she was holding an

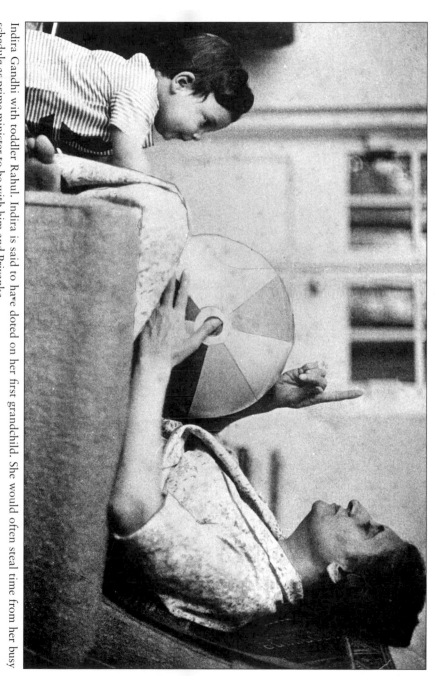

Indira Gandhi with toddler Rahul. Indira is said to have doted on her first grandchild. She would often steal time from her busy schedule as prime minister to be with him and Priyanka

Photograph courtesy Indian Express Archive

Rajiv Gandhi with a fourteen-year-old Rahul on 5 November 1984 at Teen Murti Bhavan in New Delhi, a few days after Prime Minister Indira Gandhi's death. Rajiv's prime ministership was ushered in suddenly by his mother's brutal assassination at the hands of her Sikh bodyguards on 31 October that year. His life and political career ended abruptly on 21 May 1991 at the hands of Sri Lankan Tamil insurgents. Both events affected Rahul's life significantly.

Photograph courtesy Indian Express Archive

Rahul Gandhi with Jammu and Kashmir chief minister Omar Abdullah at an election rally at Vijaypur, 35 kilometres from Jammu, in April 2009. Rahul was instrumental in Omar getting the position of chief minister of the northern Indian state, in January 2009, where the Congress and the National Conference are in a coalition. Omar's grandfather Sheikh Abdullah was a friend of Rahul's great-grandfather, Jawaharlal Nehru.
Photograph by Amarjeet Singh courtesy Indian Express Archive

Delhi Pradesh Congress Committee president, Jai Prakash Agarwal (right), offers a garland to Party general secretary Rahul Gandhi (centre) during the eighty-third plenary session of the Indian National Congress in New Delhi on 19 December 2010. Rahul used the occasion to assert the supremacy of the Party over the government and rebuked ministers for not giving enough time to party workers.
Photograph by Raul Irani

Rahul interacts with Congress president Sonia Gandhi's political secretary Ahmed Patel at the release function of the Party's manifesto on 24 March 2009 at 24 Akbar Road, New Delhi. Rahul got subject experts to make presentations to the committee drafting the manifesto so that they could get a better grip on the country's problems. In day-to-day affairs, Rahul has mostly kept his distance from the old guard in the Party represented by the likes of Patel.
Photograph courtesy Fotocorp

Rahul with Digvijaya Singh, the Congress general secretary in charge of Uttar Pradesh, and other members of his core team (in silhouette) at a congregation of Bhatta–Parsaul farmers in Greater Noida on 11 May 2011. A close adviser of Rahul, Singh has been advocating his taking over both the Party leadership and the prime minister's post for a long time.
Photograph by Ravi Choudhary

Rahul Gandhi with locals at Nangla Bhatana village about 80 kilometres from New Delhi, on 7 July 2011, during his 'Kisan Sandesh Yatra'—the three-day march on foot he led through western Uttar Pradesh. Rahul joined farmers protesting against the acquisition of their land by the state government headed by Bahujan Samaj Party chief Mayawati. The 2012 assembly election in Uttar Pradesh pitches the two against each other.
Photograph by Ashish Sharma

Rahul Gandhi inaugurated the Guru Tegh Bahadur Memorial, dedicated to the ninth Sikh guru, near the Delhi–Haryana border on 30 July 2011. He thanked the Sikhs saying, 'Prime Minister Manmohan Singh is taking the nation forward. You gave him to us and for this, the entire nation is thankful to you.' Rahul has been trying to build bridges with the community given the violent events of 1984.

Photograph by Ashish Sharma

With sister Priyanka Gandhi Vadra in New Delhi on 28 September 2011. The two distributed 220 three-wheeled scooters to the physically challenged at a programme organized by the Rajiv Gandhi Foundation. With Sonia suffering from an undisclosed ailment that required surgery in August 2011, many in the Party expect Priyanka to take the plunge into electoral politics in the next Lok Sabha election.
Photograph by Raul Irani

Prime Minister Manmohan Singh with UPA chairperson Sonia Gandhi and Rahul Gandhi shortly after Singh's government won the July 2008 trust vote. Singh has said, more than once, that he would be happy to make way for someone younger.

office of profit as chairperson of the Uttar Pradesh Film Development Council. The ruling brought into focus Sonia's several positions—as head of the NAC, the Rajiv Gandhi Foundation, the Indira Gandhi National Centre for Arts, and so on. At the time of the court's decision, Sonia held such posts in more than a dozen bodies. The budget session of Parliament was on. The Opposition began to demand Sonia's resignation as NAC chief. It stalled Parliament repeatedly saying the government would bring an ordinance to exclude the NAC chairperson's office from the list of offices of profit. The din in Parliament began to get louder. Sonia, Rahul and Priyanka discussed the situation among themselves, just as they had less than two years ago. Rahul convinced Sonia not to let the 'sacrifice of 2004' go in vain. Just as she had in May 2004, Sonia shocked the Opposition again: she resigned as NAC chairperson and Lok Sabha MP.

Reporters covering the Congress beat got an SMS from Congress secretary Tom Vadakkan on the afternoon of 23 March 2006 saying Mrs Gandhi would make an important announcement. It gave them barely fifteen minutes to react. At 10 Janpath, swarms of journalists got busy registering themselves for entry at the reception manned by the SPG. No phones were allowed inside. Sonia emerged after the journalists were ushered to the lawn outside the house. Rahul accompanied her, while Priyanka stayed inside, and she announced her resignation. She said she would go back to the people of Rae Bareli and seek their verdict.

This was the first instance after the 2006 plenary—two months to be precise—that Rahul showed signs of taking up a larger role. He offered to be Sonia's election manager for the by-election from Rae Bareli on 8 May, and his mother was only too happy to have him take up the task. Less than a month from the date of Sonia's resignation, he went and camped in Rae Bareli. Every day, in the sweltering April heat, he would address a dozen or so public meetings, halting after every few kilometres. His speeches at these public meetings, attended sometimes by just a few dozen people, were more or less identical, but seemed to strike a chord with the audience. He reminded the people of their old links with the Nehru–Gandhi family and thanked them for their unending support. He held about 300 public meetings in the short period of three weeks, while Sonia visited the constituency only for a couple of large rallies at the beginning and the end of the campaign. Priyanka, too, mostly stayed away. She came to the constituency as Sonia's election agent only at the fag end of the campaign. The mother–daughter duo were plainly happy to let Rahul take charge. Sonia won by the largest margin she had ever had. It was a multiple victory for Sonia—apart from the electoral gain and the rise in political stature, Rahul had shown the first signs of willingness to shoulder a larger responsibility. Though it was to be another year by the time he finally agreed to become the party general secretary and take charge of the youth organizations, the year 2006 did see Rahul shed some of his reluctance.

Being in charge of the Congress youth and student wings isn't the most important post at the general-secretary level. But, if anyone has any doubts about Rahul's stature in the Party, all they need to do is look carefully at the proceedings of the plenary in 2010. There were no drum-beaters and sloganeers at the meet, demanding more powers for Rahul. What more could they have asked for, anyway? Rahul was the only Congress leader other than Prime Minister Manmohan Singh—neither of them had ever been an INC president— who had his sepia-toned picture adorning a 20-foot-high stand-alone billboard along with those of Mahatma Gandhi, Jawaharlal Nehru, Sardar Patel, Sarojini Naidu, S.C. Bose and others. Besides, Prime Minister Manmohan Singh had already said earlier that year that he would be 'very happy to make place for anybody the Congress Party decides'. The brazen display of sycophancy at the

January 2006 plenary was missing in December 2010. Instead, there were subliminal signs of the demand raised in 2006—of Rahul's taking over the Party's reins—having been met with. Sonia was the president, dealing with the old guard and old allies, while Rahul was laying the path for the future and, in doing that, steering and influencing the decisions of the Party in the present. What remained to be done was his taking over as prime minister but that would happen after he had fulfilled his promise of having strengthened the Party. Till then, Congress workers and leaders, the sloganeers for putting him in charge of everything, would wait patiently.

As Congress president, Sonia Gandhi dedicated a large part of her speech to what she described as the 'democratic, professional and systematic' manner in which the IYC and the NSUI were making qualitative additions to their ranks. The Party, she said, was happy to welcome more and more young people. Despite the debacle in Bihar, where the Party has made new enemies out of old friends—Lalu Prasad Yadav's Rashtriya Janata Dal and Ram Vilas Paswan's Lok Janshakti Party—Sonia declared that Rahul's chosen line of a go-alone Congress would persist.

At Hyderabad, on returning to power after a long gap, if the Party was conscious of coalition realities and its coalition dharma, the Delhi plenary was held in an atmosphere of increasing tension between the Congress and its existing and its former allies. Taking a cue from Rahul's remarks during his tour of West Bengal in mid-2010 (when he said the Congress would respect its ally, Trinamool Congress, but wouldn't bow to it), MP Deepa Dasmunsi lashed out at the Bengal ally for not treating the Congress with enough respect. She spoke of 'conspiracies against the Congress', pleading with the Congress president not to give away seats to the allies in places where the Party was strong. Rahul's aide and former Youth Congress leader Manicka Tagore, now an MP from Tamil Nadu, took on the DMK, one of the significant allies of the Congress. He spoke of the 'self-respect of the Congress worker', and of establishing Congress rule in the southern state, echoing Rahul's remarks. The general secretary in charge of UP and Assam, Digvijaya Singh, suggested in his speech that it was time for not just Rahul but his entire team to take over the Party. Digvijaya Singh announced after his passionate bashing of the BJP and the RSS, that he and the likes of Ahmed Patel (Sonia Gandhi's political secretary), Ghulam Nabi Azad (former Jammu and Kashmir chief minister and party general secretary) and Ashok Gehlot (the reigning Rajasthan chief minister) had been brought in by Rajiv Gandhi when they were in their mid-thirties. 'Now, our expiry date is nearing,' he said, adding, 'I am confident Rahul Gandhi will make his own team.'

As for Rahul himself, the period between the two plenaries saw him slowly taking charge of things. From being a low-key first-time MP, to being Sonia Gandhi's election manager, to determining the course of the Congress alliances, he had come a long way. This time around, in his speech, he even took on ministers in the Manmohan Singh government for not doing enough for party workers, or taking time out, during their visits, to meet party functionaries. 'The organization is the bridge between the government and the people. There are ministers and chief ministers here on stage. You should give more time to the party workers. Wherever I go, I hear this complaint,' he announced from the dais. The tent, filled with delegates—AICC members from all over the country, members of the frontal organizations like the Congress Seva Dal and the All India Mahila Congress— broke into a thunderous applause as Rahul gently rebuked the ministers seated on the raised platform.

He spoke of linking the common man's life with the growth engine of the country's economy. Of course, Rahul's address had its emotional appeal this time as well.

'Anyone not connected to the system' is the common man, he said.

> We call him the common man but, in fact, he is unique. He has immense capabilities, intelligence and strength. He builds this country every day of his life and yet our system crushes him at every step. We will never build a nation until we build a system in which this man's progress is based not on whom he knows but on what he knows. This is the challenge for our generation.

Rahul had prevailed upon the Congress to replace the 'poor man' with the 'common man' as the chief beneficiary of the Party's promised policies in its 2004 pitch when it was attempting to come back to power. In 2010, he set out to define who this common man was. He cut a wide swathe by including the country's ever-growing middle class.

12 Tughlaq Lane

Within the Congress, a peculiar insecurity preceded the Lok Sabha elections of 2009. Allies went their own ways, leaving the Congress jittery about its chances of returning to power. It was hard to find anyone in the grand old party smiling. Unless, of course, they were on camera. The older the leader, the more resigned he was to the prospect of the Party's not crossing the one-third mark in the Lok Sabha tally. An internal survey of the Congress said it was going to emerge as the single largest party. But the survey pegged the number of seats in the Congress kitty at just about 150. The level of self-doubt in the Congress ranks was rather high. Even among those who worked with Rahul, it was only the young and the less experienced who were convinced that the Party would do better than it had done in the previous election. That most of them had acquired their political education outside the electoral arena added to the worries of experienced Congressmen.

Open magazine pegged the number at 165 seats. The magazine's political bureau, where one of the authors of this book works, had looked at the state-wise condition of the Congress, and come up with that figure, which was published in the run-up to the 2009 election. 'You are either being too nice to us or you can see something that we in the Congress can't,' said a Congressman who is an old associate of the family and is one of those who handle the activities of the Rajiv Gandhi Foundation in Rae Bareli and Amethi. '*Agar aisa ho jaye to apke munh mein ghee shakkar* (If we can pull that off, may you be blessed),' he said with scepticism, sitting in his makeshift office at the Congress headquarters in New Delhi.

In such a scenario, the move to go it alone, and by alienating key allies, would be disastrous, Congressmen with more salt than pepper in their hair told each other. At 24 Akbar Road—the Party headquarters and a lesser centre of power after 10 Janpath—many argued that the Congress ought to learn from the BJP's 2004 experience.

The BJP, which had ruled the country from 1998 to 2004 as the head of a motley alliance of parties, had finished with 138 seats in the 2004 elections. That was just seven MPs fewer than the Congress's 145 but it could not muster another alliance to return to power. Another chief cause of worry for Congress party leaders was the falling out between the UPA and the Left. For more than four years, different constituents of the Left Bloc comprising over sixty MPs led by the Communist Part of India (Marxist) had backed the UPA. The Left had supported the Congress-led government from outside and lent the much-needed stability to the coalition government. In 2008, however, the Left and the Congress drifted apart on the issue of the Indo-US nuclear deal, ultimately leading to the Left's withdrawal of outside support to the UPA government. They fought the 2009 election with the bitterness of former partners who have just been through a divorce.

In short, the mood was that of uncertainty. The Party was going to the polls, after five years in power, unsure of which way the voter would swing, and therefore, sceptical of returning to form a government. But, if you had looked where cameras were forbidden, and still are, you would have spotted a completely different atmosphere: the young and very business-like Team RG was busy at work. The members of the team appeared to be filled with a sense of purpose—something that they seemed to have acquired from their leader. They were working to a plan, based on their own little inputs and everything he had picked up over the years. They organized his election tours meticulously, ignoring reports of the Congress's barely satisfactory prospects. While the seniors in the Party harboured mixed feelings, this team of young people was sure of the Congress improving on its previous tally. Call it lack of experience or political acumen (a quality that often manifests itself as cynicism), or the necessary caution so characteristic of experienced politicians, the team around Rahul worked unmindful of the pitfalls of pushing him into an election that—based on the Party's own assessment—the Congress might lose.

Confident of the Party's prospects, Rahul clocked more than 85,000 kilometres in election travel, campaigning and speaking tirelessly. If he was addressing an election rally in Punjab's Hoshiarpur, the event would be preceded by one at Tiruchirapalli in Tamil Nadu, and followed by another at Roorkee in Uttarakhand. At the end of the campaign, he had addressed over a 110 rallies and touched almost every state in the country. By the time the election results came in, it was clear that Team

RG had struck gold. The Congress finished with a higher tally than it had in 2004. Quite a few of the foot soldiers even returned from the election battlefield as members of the Lok Sabha.

With its headquarters at 12 Tughlaq Lane—the house officially allotted to Rahul Gandhi as the MP from Amethi—the team has been slowly preparing the curriculum for the future. The election win of 2009 was firmly tucked away in the trophy showcase. At forty-one years of age, Rahul can afford to be patient. 'I am still young,' he had said during the 2009 campaign. In his view, short opportunistic alliances to gain power had weakened the Party. 'We would have liked alliances with Mulayam Singhji, Laluji and Paswanji to keep the secular vote intact, but their attitude disappointed us. The Party will only benefit from going it alone in the long run,' said Congress general secretary Digvijaya Singh in the run-up to the general election. 'The Party went through a series of flip-flops after 1991, supporting one party or the other, and that proved disastrous,' he added, laying down what could be expected in the near future: 'The result is that we have to start building it from scratch in certain parts.'

A slow change that will be for the long haul. The databanks being monitored and the spreadsheets being pored over by Team RG—all these activities do convey the message that this is a management project. There are hints of changes taking place at a faster pace. The Rahul Gandhi Corporation has its work cut out, more so after the successes of 2009. After the UPA's almost surprising win in May 2009 that brought the economist prime minister Manmohan Singh back to power, the team's task has become even more daunting. It must deliver a bigger, better and more confident leader to succeed Dr Singh as India's next prime minister in 2014. Not just that; the Party's tally in the next general election should be even more impressive than the 206 seats of 2009 so as to make governance easier or, at least, the decision-making more effective. 'RG is not in a hurry. He says we have a twenty-year game plan and that his goal is to tap the youth,' revealed a close aide. Rahul, at a meeting with young professionals, said, 'Give me ten years of your life and at the end of those ten years, you will be very proud of what you have achieved.' He was out on one of his talent hunts scouting for educated young men and women to bring into politics. The big question, however, is whether professionals from the 'I-want-it-yesterday' world would have the patience to wait and to achieve such long-term goals. Probably not. The point to note here is that the strategy for shaping the Party's future is not being devised at 10 Janpath, India's most important address, but at 12 Tughlaq Lane.

Ironically, this emerging power centre is located on a street named after a dynasty brought down by its last scion's futuristic ideas. Back in the fourteenth century, Muhammad bin Tughlaq dreamt of a pan-Indian sultanate, launched token currency and shifted base for better strategic control. Large-scale counterfeiting, famines, opposition from the orthodoxy and a rebellion jeopardized his grand plans. Rahul, too, has brought in ideas considered out-of-sync with the times, and whether his fate will be any different from that of Tughlaq will depend on the outcome of his efforts. The Congress tally in the 2009 general elections silenced critics, but only for a short while.

The emphasis on youth has been just the start. Team RG's first task was to rejuvenate the IYC and the NSUI. Since September 2007, when Rahul took charge of the two units, lakhs of new members have been signed up. 'The pace at which things were moving, we could see the IYC touching a figure of over one crore by the time the drive ended,' said Ashok Tanwar, Congress MP from Sirsa, Haryana, in 2009. Tanwar was the IYC president in 2007 when Rahul took over as the general secretary steering the two outfits, a post previously held by his father Rajiv and uncle Sanjay. The target for membership was later revised to two crores for the IYC and the NSUI put together. By mid-2011, the IYC decided to extend its membership drive and make it a continuing process. Punjab, for instance, conducted a second round of recruitments that year.

Youth empowerment is the team's KRA (key result area)—a goal etched in stone. To Rahul's credit, the IYC and the NSUI conducted internal elections for the very first time, and the talent hunts have lapped up youngsters with fire in their bellies. But such hunts haven't always been without trouble. In Kerala, in 2009, for instance, M. Liju, Rahul's choice as Youth Congress president, had to be sacked within hours of his appointment, as a measure to quell a local rebellion. In 2010, serious allegations against the Youth Congress president of the Goa state unit threatened to snowball into a full-blown controversy. A district president wrote to the IYC top brass and Rahul alleging that the state committee was involved in siphoning money from a flood relief fund. He later said he was removed from his post in the Youth Congress and his allegations were not pursued. No inquiry was conducted and he ended up quitting the Party.

* * *

The Congress had never seen anything like 12 Tughlaq Lane before. An aide of Rahul Gandhi's said, 'The functioning of the office is completely professional.' He cited an example to underline the changes that took place in the IYC control room after Rahul took charge. Rahul was to go to Puducherry on 25 March 2009 on the eve of the general election. But his visit would have clashed with the schedule of IYC local chapter. The Puducherry unit e-mailed Tanwar's office about the problem. The e-mail was forwarded immediately to 12 Tughlaq Lane, where Sachin Rao, who looks after the youth organizations, checked with Kanishka Singh and got back to the Puducherry Youth Congress office within minutes. Rahul's visit was rescheduled. 'The entire office runs on BlackBerry,' confided a team member. The joke in Congress circles is that one reason why the Government of India went soft on BlackBerry service despite security and encryption problems is because the IYC and the NSUI—and, ultimately, the overhaul of the Congress—are fashioned around it. Compare this to 24 Akbar Road where the broadcast vans of TV channels parked outside offer the only hint of modernity.

Kanishka Singh, who is younger than Rahul by six years, is a Wharton MBA. The son of S.K. Singh, a former governor and an old Rajiv Gandhi associate, he quit his job as an investment banker with Lazard Frères & Co. in New York to join the Congress. In an early 2004 article in *Outlook* magazine, drawing parallels between Indian general elections and American presidential polls, Kanishka Singh had likened Sonia Gandhi to John Kerry and predicted wins for both. He was only half-right but that was really the half that mattered. He has been an integral part of Team RG since. In another essay published in 2005 in *Seminar*, Kanishka (or K, as they call him in the team) pushed for doing away with the gerontocracy that rules India in favour of dynamic leadership. He argued that most influential leaders in both the BJP and the Congress would be either over the hill or approaching the point from where a decline is inevitable. Dr Manmohan Singh, seventy-eight years old in 2010, would not be pitched again as the Party's prime ministerial candidate in 2014. That's a well-established fact within and outside Congress circles. Arjun Singh at eighty (he died on 4 March 2011) had already retired from active politics, Sonia Gandhi at sixty-four was only too eager to pass on the mantle to her son—Kanishka Singh argued in his thesis. He reasoned that, with Vajpayee turning eighty-six and Advani eighty-three in 2010, a generational shift in the BJP would be absolutely necessary:

The writing is on the wall with regard to a generational shift in the BJP by 2010. The Vajpayee–Advani duo will no longer be at the helm of that party five years from now. The jury is still out on who could possibly grow into that role in the BJP. The Congress, too, must see some turnover in its senior ranks by 2010. However, the near-universal ageing of the Party's entire senior leadership rung shall not have taken place, unlike in the BJP. Smaller national and regional parties, too, are witnessing generational shifts with the passing of the baton. The period between now and 2010 is likely to herald a partial dismantling of the gerontocracy that India has evolved into during the post-Rajiv Gandhi era. A younger leadership in India will, by default, have the ability to think and act beyond a limited five-year time horizon. The potential upside of such a shift is considerable.

The 'younger leadership' referred to by Kanishka is clearly Rahul Gandhi, the exemplar of dynamism in the Congress world view.

Compare this with what Digvijaya Singh—chief minister of Madhya Pradesh for two consecutive terms till 2003—told his interviewer, Hartosh Singh Bal (*Tehelka*, 11 June 2005):

Every political party has to build up new leadership. In the 1960s, Indira Gandhiji picked up a number of young people who became chief ministers in the states, ministers in the state and Central government and important functionaries in the AICC. In the 1970s, Sanjay Gandhi did the same thing and then in the 1980s Rajivji picked up people like Ashok Gehlot and Ahmed Patel. I was made PCC president in Madhya Pradesh at the age of 37.

This kind of generational change has to take place, and we would like Rahul Gandhi to come to the organization as soon as possible so that the most challenging task today—the process of building up from grassroots to the AICC—is done by a whole set of younger people. It may take some time but the process of generational change within the Congress party has to start . . . I strongly feel the new team must have Rahul Gandhi as general secretary of the AICC so that youth could be given predominance at all levels of the organization.

We have to slowly build up our own cadre and more so when we have to face the challenge of the BJP in some states and the Left Front in some other states. The Congress has always been more or less a mass-based party and not a cadre-based party. But both the BJP and the Left Front are cadre-based. We not only have to build cadres but also instil discipline in the Party.

Of course, Digvijaya Singh would repeat these assertions at different fora, including the Congress Party's plenary sessions. He said this as early as mid-2005, and changes in the Congress seem to have followed this pattern. Digvijaya remains among Rahul's closest advisers from the Congress old guard, while Kanishka has, over the years, emerged as his closest confidant outside the Gandhi family.

Kanishka Singh's proximity to Rahul allows him to get his ideas across more often than not. He also prepares Rahul's daily schedule and clears appointments. 'He is Rahul's Man Friday,' revealed a source from within the set-up, 'the real shadow, who goes with him everywhere and sits next to him in the aircraft on all official trips.' To get through to Rahul, you have to go through Kanishka. He is equally at ease in Hindi and English, and he is the man who screens the leader's office mail and gets in touch with those who need to be contacted. The list can sometimes include chief ministers and corporate heads.

When Akhilesh Das, Rajya Sabha MP and former minister of state for steel, quit the Congress in May 2008 to join Mayawati, he blamed the 'coterie around Rahul Gandhi' in his letter to Sonia. The disgruntled Das went on to allege that Kanishka Singh's father was appointed Rajasthan governor despite being close to the BJP because of his proximity to the Congress's generation next.

The team's management wonk, Sachin Rao, is closer to his boss in age. He was in the software solutions business before getting an MBA from the Michigan Business School in corporate strategy and international business. A project with management guru C.K. Prahalad turned Rao's interest towards poverty and the possibility of looking at the bottom of the pyramid (BoP)—the vast base of India's socio-economic structure—as a viable opportunity that has been ignored. After a couple of farm sector projects with multinationals, he joined the Centre for Civil Society in Delhi. Soon, he was spotted by Rahul, whose own exploration of the 'real' India—visiting Dalit homes in Amethi and hauling bricks along with labourers in Rajasthan—drew lessons from Rao's experience in understanding poverty.

In the Congress organization, there are many others on whom Rahul relies. Congress secretaries Jitendra Singh and Meenakshi Natarajan, both Rahul's age, have worked closely with him in overseeing the affairs of the IYC and the NSUI, respectively. Jitendra, a royal from

Alwar in Rajasthan, studied engineering in Germany, and was twice elected as Congress MLA from Alwar before joining the team. He is now the party's Lok Sabha MP from Alwar and, since July 2011, a junior minister in the crucial ministry of home affairs. Rahul ensured that both Jitendra and Meenakshi got tickets for the Lok Sabha elections of 2009, as he did for Tanwar and Manicka Tagore, who are also part of the 12 Tughlaq Lane clique.

Tanwar came to the Lok Sabha by winning the election from Sirsa, the home ground of former Haryana chief minister Om Prakash Chautala. Tagore is a school-teacher's son who rose from the ranks of the NSUI to the IYC and ultimately to Parliament defeating the virulent Marumalarchi Dravida Munnetra Kazhagam (MDMK) chief and known LTTE supporter Vaiyapuri Gopalasamy (also known as Vaiko) in his own backyard.

Meenakshi did an MSc in Biochemistry and got a law degree from Indore before taking the plunge as a career politician. She is now the Congress MP from Mandsaur in Madhya Pradesh, a traditional BJP stronghold. Though her parents are Tamil, Meenakshi was born and brought up in Madhya Pradesh and is fluent in Hindi. Her father, a railway employee, moved to the central Indian state from their home town in Tamil Nadu.

There is something remarkable about the way in which these young men and women, handpicked by Rahul Gandhi, have won seats against formidable opponents. While making electoral choices, voters, it seems, were willing to give youth a chance over more traditional attributes. This understanding is also to a very large extent the base on which Team RG is formulating its future plans. The young MPs are completely engrossed in building the youth units of the Party into formidable fortresses that will help the Congress fight Opposition parties. But their performance as legislators has been rather poor.

Consider this: Jitendra and Meenakshi have done nothing much when it comes to participation in parliamentary proceedings or law-making. Till the end of the budget session of 2010, Jitendra had participated in only two debates and asked no questions of the ministries. Meenakshi had participated in just three debates and posed five questions. Ashok Tanwar rose to political prominence within the Congress student circles, and became NSUI president for establishing the student body's presence in Jawaharlal Nehru University (JNU). But, since being elected to the Lok Sabha in 2009, Tanwar has shown no signs of his alma mater's culture of debating every issue under the sun. He had not participated in a single debate till the end of the 2010 monsoon session of the lower house. Nor had he bothered to ask a single question. By contrast, the average MP has asked an average of 62 questions in the 15th Lok Sabha till May 2010 and participated in 8.6 debates.

Note that the IYC and the NSUI are the foundations for Rahul Gandhi's grand plan of tapping youth power for a stronger, stand-alone Congress and, ultimately, for nation-building. The programmes of these two organizations highlight the need for youth to participate in politics, but the MPs in charge of these programmes may not be setting the best examples on what to do after a young man or a woman does make it to Parliament.

Meanwhile, the relationships that his father Rajiv Gandhi nurtured have been renewed. Sam Pitroda, who ushered in Rajiv's telecom revolution and is currently chairman of the National Knowledge Commission, is a key adviser. Jairam Ramesh, who was minister of state for commerce in UPA-I and became environment minister and, later, rural development minister in UPA-II, arranged most of Rahul's interactions with experts in the field and outside the government. During the first run of the UPA, cabinet minister Mani Shankar Aiyar helped Rahul by drawing on his own experience of working in the government, and as a bureaucrat and a diplomat. The idea was to keep the prime-minister-in-training engaged not only with the Indian heartland, but with things happening elsewhere in the world. On questions of how prime ministerial authority is effectively exercised, Rahul relied on Prithviraj Chavan, former minister of state in the PMO (the prime minister's office). Chavan was later appointed Maharashtra chief minister. Few Congressmen doubt that this elaborate exercise (of educating a PM probable) is merely a matter of curiosity. Perhaps, Rahul Gandhi would do well to ponder one of the dictums of Harvard, a place of brief sojourn in his journey: Never confuse the idea of authority with the authority of ideas. For, apart from resisting the label of a dynast, he has to fight the irony of his address—Tughlaq Lane.

Youth Express

On 13 August 2010, the monsoon session of Parliament was under way. Both houses were in session that Friday. But elsewhere in the Parliament House complex, in the annexe to be precise, a rare exercise was taking place: an eight-hour training session for a select group of young and emerging Congress leaders, including four dozen MLAs and MPs from all over the country.

Szarita Laitphlang spent most of the day at the session. The previous evening, she had been shopping for her ten-year-old son who was studying at a boarding school in Assam. He was home, in Kolkata, on vacation. 'I have to catch the morning flight. He will be sleeping when I get home,' she said, her eyes sparkling with excitement and longing. The excitement was in anticipation of the three days she would spend with her son. There was also fatigue etched on her face probably as a result of the long session she had just attended, and the realization that, at the end of the three-day break, she would have to plunge into her new assignment as one of the Congress Party's coordinators in the coming West Bengal elections. All forty-two of the young MLAs who attended the session were also bound for West Bengal. Each was in charge of a particular territory in the eastern state for the 2011 assembly elections and was also responsible, at the same time, for setting the tone for the state Youth Congress elections.

On the same day, Vijay Inder Singla, Lok Sabha MP from Sangrur, explained the IYC's new election model to the assembled MLAs. He told them about the wave of democracy that was silently sweeping through the Congress youth outfits, the IYC and the NSUI. Around the same time, these young MLAs were also witnessing the organizational elections within the Party. These elections, however, were only in name. That Sonia Gandhi would again be party president was a foregone conclusion. (Sonia was re-elected Congress president for a record fourth term on 3 September 2010. With that she became the longest-serving chief of the Indian National Congress.)

At the state level, elections in the Congress are held by consensus or by passing a one-line resolution authorizing the Congress president to nominate the state party chief. The consensus, too, is directed by New Delhi. That is the culture of the Congress. But, as these MLAs learnt at the meeting, the IYC's democratization was a process aimed at changing that culture. In contrast to the parent Congress, the IYC adopted the new election model in 2008 and, in December, Singla became the first state-level president to be replaced through an election. He went on to contest the 2009 Lok Sabha elections, getting a ticket at Rahul Gandhi's behest. He defeated his heavyweight opponent, former union minister Sukhdev Singh Dhindsa of the Shiromani Akali Dal. Dhindsa had won his first election and become a legislator in 1972, the year Singla was born.

The training session in the Parliament complex, where Singla was one of the main speakers, was a prelude to the MLAs' tour of West Bengal. Szarita would travel ahead of them and be a part of the team that organized public meetings for Rahul in early and mid-September 2010 and, along with these rallies, the IYC's membership drive. The entire process would consume three months. 'Then I will get to meet my son again,' she added. Since most politicians work long hours, one could ask, what was so different in her case? Well, for one, Szarita wasn't even a Congress member yet. She was thirty-three and just a part of the IYC. Except for the brief period in which the IYC was talked about, and infamously so, under Sanjay Gandhi, it had just been a place for politicians' kids to hang out in before they were old enough to be in the grand old party. But now, Rahul Gandhi had begun using it as a tool to set the stage for inner party democracy in the Congress.

Rajeev Satav, IYC president and Maharashtra MLA, who had also been present at the training session, said he would probably be the last nominated president of the youth outfit: 'The nomination culture is changing.' The IYC was attracting fresh blood. 'The election process that is on will change the IYC forever. Nominations were replaced by elections in 2008. By the time we finish the IYC membership drive and elections, we will have about two crore IYC members with their own elected representatives at various levels,' Satav added.

Before the end of 2011, the IYC hoped to finish the first round of its recruitment and election process in all the states and union territories. 'We will have a large pool of dedicated young men and women without a criminal background, raring to go,' said Singla. Rahul Gandhi had entrusted Singla with the task of overseeing the elections to the IYC as an 'election commissioner'.

The IYC elections make for a tedious process. Several weeks pass between the beginning of the membership drive and the completion of the elections. Membership is opened for thirty days. Those who apply are screened for criminal antecedents by FAME—the Foundation for Advanced Management of Elections—formed by the likes of former chief election commissioners J.M. Lyngdoh and N. Gopalaswami, and former adviser to the Election Commission K.J. Rao. After the scrutiny is over, elections take place at the gram panchayat or municipal ward level. Then follow the assembly- and state-level elections.

'Until FAME endorses it, the election is null and void,' explained Singla. The first election was held in December 2008 in Punjab. Rahul himself supervised it with Lyngdoh and K.J. Rao. The election resulted in Ravneet Singh Bittu, grandson of assassinated Punjab chief minister Beant Singh, being elected as the new president. Bittu was backed by one former chief minister, and his opponent by another. Despite the elaborate exercise in democracy, a dynast had emerged as the new president. But in the process, the state Youth Congress got itself over three lakh new members. 'That was the first election,' said Singla, adding, 'As awareness of the process spreads, we have more numbers enrolling for membership and more first-timers coming to the fore.' He had just come back after supervising the Bihar Youth Congress elections in the first week of August 2010. To underline the effectiveness of the process initiated by the election system, Congress leaders cited the example of Lallan Kumar, the new Bihar Youth Congress president who did not belong to a political family.

There are many others who are first-timers in politics with no political lineage or baggage. Szarita's family, for instance, runs a small business in Shillong and she studied English literature at St. Mary's Convent in Shillong before getting herself a Microsoft certification as a software professional. But things changed when she was picked up in the talent search conducted by Rahul Gandhi and his associates before the election process began. A Khasi tribal from Meghalaya, she was appointed national coordinator of the IYC's Aam Aadmi ka Sipahi (AAKS: the common man's foot soldier) initiative for the North-east. Ten districts of Assam were chosen for the pilot programme which was formally launched by Rahul Gandhi in July 2009. The AAKS hoped to push thousands of new IYC recruits into the rural hinterland and become the Congress's main plank of social participation and engagement with the poor. But it never went beyond the pilot stage.

Abdul Hafiz Gandhi, a former national secretary of the IYC, comes from that background—rural and poor. He belongs to Mou village in the Patiyali assembly constituency of what was once Etah but has been renamed Kanshiram Nagar by the Mayawati government. Abdul's father is a marginal farmer, tilling five bighas of land in the village. His uncle was a cement contractor and he helped Abdul move to Delhi at the age of six in the hope of a better future. From the village school, Abdul moved to an English-medium school in an east Delhi locality. 'At that time, I spoke no English and even my Hindi dialect was the butt of jokes,' he recalled. One glance at his Facebook profile and you know he has come a long way since then. 'Whenever I go back home, I travel to the villages in my area and meet the people there. They are very poor. I want to do something for them. That is why I have chosen politics as a career,' he said.

After an integrated five-year Bachelor of Law degree from the Aligarh Muslim University (AMU), Abdul could have become a lawyer and pulled his family out of poverty. Instead, he completed his masters and then chose to pursue an MPhil and a PhD on scholarship at

Delhi's Jawaharlal Nehru University. His research involves assessing the impact of the Right to Information Act, a key showcase legislation of UPA-I.

'When I was at AMU, I filed a case in the Supreme Court seeking the restoration of the students' union there. The SC dismissed my plea but we started an agitation. The vice chancellor agreed to our demand and I became the students' union president in 2005,' said Abdul. Spurred by the success of the agitation, he entered student politics and decided to study further. 'Despite being the union president, I topped the JNU entrance exam for MPhil,' he said to underscore the point that political and academic success need not be mutually exclusive. In 2009 and early 2010, Abdul toured Madhya Pradesh to do the spadework for the IYC elections to be held in late 2010. His work in Madhya Pradesh done, Abdul was moved to Jharkhand with a similar brief: to prepare the ground for the Youth Congress elections there. On his way back from Jamshedpur to New Delhi in September 2010, he took the opportunity to visit his native Patiyali constituency which had been hit by floods. He wants to contest the 2012 assembly election from there.

True to Rahul Gandhi's formula of preparing the ground early, Abdul began preparations for the elections in 2009. He walked through his constituency, covering village after village, meeting people in their homes and shops. By the end of 2010, he had a list of thousands of voters in his constituency with details such as their addresses, mobile phone numbers, occupation, details of the family and income. 'These days, most people carry a cell phone. When I hold a public meeting, I send messages to people who live within a few kilometres of the venue. As a result, the numbers in public meetings have been slowly growing,' he said. Since the 2009 elections, Abdul has had simple slogans painted on a few walls in Patiyali along with his name. *'Congress ke Saath Judein* (Get associated with the Congress)—Abdul Hafiz Gandhi,' says one. Every year after the monsoons, he gets those slogans repainted. By the time the election code of conduct kicks in for the 2012 polls and bars such slogans, Abdul's efforts will have registered with the locals.

Abdul is one of the few people who started early, cashing in on the stupendous performance of the Congress in the state in the 2009 Lok Sabha elections. From being a fringe player in the state, the Congress bounced back to finish second in the tally. Though he wasn't even sure that he would get to contest the 2012 assembly elections on a Congress ticket, Abdul launched the preparations for an electoral plunge. Abdul's strategy is a strong counter to Mayawati's Bahujan Samaj Party—a party that announces a majority of its candidates several months before the elections. But the bad news for the Congress is that there aren't too many such young men and women in the state who have begun preparing for future electoral battles.

Traditionally, the Congress, unlike Mayawati, waits and declares candidates for elections just a few days, or even hours, before the deadline for filing the nomination papers ends. The Party's managers keep putting off declaring their candidates till the very end in the hope that those who are denied tickets will not enter the election as candidates of other political parties. Often such contenders who are denied tickets, contest the election as independents—and sometimes even win. Dealing with a rebel who contests the election as an independent is perhaps easier than dealing with someone who joins another political party and enters the fray. But there are those in the Congress who argue that rebels who enter the political arena even as independents, while incapable of winning on their own, do spoil the game. They wean votes away from the Party's official candidate and cause electoral upsets.

In August 2011, egged on by Rahul Gandhi's UP 2012 formula, the Congress tried to break away from the eleventh-hour principle and started declaring candidates for the UP polls. Before the month ended, the Party had announced its first list of seventy-three candidates who would contest the election in 2012 on the party ticket. Rahul, along with Prime Minister Manmohan Singh, presided over the Party's election committee meeting at which the list was cleared.

Like Abdul, Szarita is serious about politics. 'At some point of time, I do want to be an elected representative, whether at the state or the national level,' she said. She hopes to contest the 2013 assembly polls in her state. The decision to become a career politician had begun to take shape when she joined the Youth Congress in 2006 in her home town of Shillong. But, it was only in October 2008 that she felt she had taken the right decision. On 2 October 2008, Szarita was in Bordubi Gaon in the Madhuban area of the Tinsukia constituency in Assam as part of AAKS.

AAKS activists all over the country had been asked to go to the remotest of villages and do physical labour (*shramdaan*). It was an apparent tribute to Mahatma Gandhi and, at the same time, a good way of connecting with the poor in the remote villages. Rahul Gandhi himself participated in one such programme at Amroli village in Kota district of Rajasthan that day, hauling soil in metal and plastic pans. Of course, Rahul's participation in the shramdaan made it to the headlines the next day and so did his statement. 'Every single day, I feel there are two Indias. One that lives in the cities and belongs to the rich; the other India is that of the poor. We have to connect these two,' he had famously remarked after the programme.

Meanwhile, back in Bordubi Gaon, Szarita's team stopped at the hut of a family of tea plantation workers. It was a very poor family. Of late, an unwritten rule in the IYC is that, when working in a village, volunteers must eat with the poorest families. 'We were carrying the rations to cook and we asked them for utensils. The village had been recently electrified but the house did not have a connection. There was a young woman in the family who was in the last month of her pregnancy. So I spoke with the local state Youth Congress and asked them to help the family with the electricity connection. I assured the family that we would try our best and left the village,' recalled Szarita. A fortnight later, when she was again in that village, she went back to the house. They had got a connection under the Kutir Jyoti Yojana—a rural electrification scheme run by the Congress government in Assam. The young woman who had been pregnant was now a mother. And the family had named the baby girl after Szarita. 'At that time, I was completely overwhelmed by the gesture. I felt so good about being in politics,' Szarita said.

What Szarita had done for the family was simple: she got a poor household something that was legitimately theirs under an existing centrally sponsored government scheme. Only, they didn't know it belonged to them. The Youth Congress team acted as a catalyst. AAKS was a programme fashioned around this disconnect. Rahul Gandhi hoped there would be millions of young men and women in their twenties and early thirties acting as catalysts between the Congress's *aam aadmi* and the establishment, winning friends for the Congress and influencing voters. The grand old party, on the other hand, would have managed to tap the largest pool of young Indians. Apart from the IYC's projected one crore members, there would be a similar number of NSUI members. The students' body, too, is in the midst of a similar drive. 'India has the world's largest pool of young people. Between two general elections, about five to seven crore voters between the age group of eighteen and twenty-three are being added. If, as a political party, we do not tap them, we are not doing our job,' said Sanjay Bapna, who was the AICC secretary in charge of the IYC till the younger Jitendra Singh replaced him.

Within three months of taking charge of the IYC and the NSUI, Rahul had set out on a talent hunt to identify young men and women who could be groomed into future leaders. At a joint meeting of the NSUI and the IYC in New Delhi on 17 November 2007, Rahul made an impassioned speech that would set the agenda in the days that followed:

It is we, the youth, who have the greatest stake in our future. It is from among the youth that tomorrow's leaders will rise. I firmly believe that the Youth Congress and the NSUI should become the vehicles for young Indians who want to serve the nation. Over the last few weeks, I have spent many hours with our workers and office-bearers. I am proud to say that there are many among them with talent, character and the will to serve. But there is work to be done. In my travels, I am often asked two questions: the first is from young people who ask me how can we join politics and help India? The second question, which comes from within the Youth Congress and the NSUI is, how do we progress within the organization? These two questions touch the heart of what needs to be changed. If we are truly to become an organization to represent the youth of our country, if we are truly to develop leaders of whom this nation can be proud, we need to do two things: The first is to build an organization that is open and relevant to the broad range of Indians who believe in our values and seek to serve the nation. The second is to build a meritocratic organization. Young people bring tremendous passion and energy into our organization. We must see to it that they are accountable. It is our duty to ensure that their progress is linked to their performance. I urge every young Indian to join us and help us build institutions worthy of your dreams, your values and your capabilities.

Rahul, and his men—Kanishka Singh and Sachin Rao, his lieutenants who work out of the MP's official residence at 12 Tughlaq Lane; Jitendra Singh who was in charge of the IYC (till he became minister of state for home affairs in the UPA government on 12 July 2011); Ashok Tanwar, MP from Sirsa in Haryana and a member of RG's core team; and the young MPs Jyotiraditya Scindia, Sachin Pilot, Jitin Prasada and Deepender Hooda—set out to tour the country and interview people. Scindia, Pilot and Prasada—all political dynasts—were later made junior ministers.

As a young MP who was part of the initial talent hunt said:

Mr Gandhi told us that even before he became an MP or the general secretary in charge, the young people he met anywhere would say they wanted to do something for the country or society but felt that politics wasn't the path they wanted to take. They felt that there was little reward for people who were honest, and that first-timers with no lineage were bound to fail sooner than later.

Through the many interactions that he had with young people, Rahul told his associates, he had learnt that young men and women were full of idealism and patriotism. Only, they were completely disillusioned with politics. So, the first step was to spread the word that those who were willing and deserving should come forward to be a part of Rahul Gandhi's large team of young leaders who would usher in the revolution in politics for which they so desperately yearned. In almost every state, young people were asked to land up at IYC-organized conclaves or meetings. There were many who said their voices were never heard. The responsibility given to youngsters did not match their talent because the children and relatives of existing politicians lapped up the top posts in every set-up, at all levels. Where there was responsibility, there was no evaluation and, finally, no reward. 'RG's thought process evolved through the meetings he had with students and young people during his travels. We had brainstorming sessions with him and people in the organization and, finally, the plan for building a democratic IYC and NSUI was formed,' the MP added.

The talent hunt used a special software to judge the applicants on several counts on a scale of one to ten: level of commitment, organizational skills, personality, past experience of social service, loyalty to the Congress, vision, ideological leanings and educational qualifications. The perfect Congressman or Congresswoman would do exceedingly well on all counts. The idea was to find as many committed young people as possible and steer them towards higher scores. 'The result of the talent hunt is that RG's office has a list of thousands of young men and women who fit the bill. They can be future leaders. Many of them have already been roped in at various levels. This is highly talented human capital that would be the envy of any large organization,' said Ashok Tanwar, who was IYC president for five years, from 2005 to the beginning of 2010. He saw his term being split into two phases: the pre-Rahul phase till September 2007 and the period that followed Rahul's appointment.

Before Rahul took over as the man in charge, the IYC was full of dead wood. Office bearers in many state units were men well past the upper-age limit for retaining an IYC membership—thirty-five. 'Over two-thirds of India's population is under thirty-five. If we wanted to attract young crowds, we had to get younger people to lead the organization,' Tanwar reasoned. Tanwar's team at the IYC office on Raisina Road drew up a list of state unit presidents who were to be changed. Many were older than Rahul, who was thirty-seven at that time and thus ineligible for membership himself. The list included sitting and past MLAs and MPs. Sukhwinder Singh Sukhu was an MLA from Himachal Pradesh and had been president of the Himachal Pradesh Youth Congress since 1998. He was forty-one years old. His Andhra Pradesh counterpart, T. Venkata Rao, also an MLA, was nearing forty. Others prominent on the list were Karnataka Youth Congress chief and second-term MLA Dinesh Gundu Rao, and Chhattisgarh's Devvrat Singh, another second-term MLA who had even contested the Lok Sabha polls. In the cleaning-up exercise that began just before Rahul took over, the overaged presidents of Haryana and Punjab were changed.

Bapna, who was then in charge of the IYC, said the Congress was looking seriously at making the IYC set-up young and vibrant once again.

The Congress president is keen that those who are over age or have been in these posts for a few years be removed to make way for the younger lot. The upper-age limit for Youth Congress posts was always thirty-five but, over the years, it was ignored. Now, we are getting things back on track.

Bapna usually took orders from his boss Sonia Gandhi, but these orders had come from Rahul. Within weeks of his taking over from Oscar Fernandes, a Rajiv Gandhi loyalist, Rahul and his team were working on the new election model for the IYC and the NSUI. The talent hunt, too, had been kicked off.

Both Szarita and Abdul emerged from the talent hunt. But Devendra Pratap Singh Patel of Satna in Madhya Pradesh was not so lucky. He had studied to be a lawyer at the APS University in Rewa and was national secretary of the Samajwadi Party's youth wing, the Yuvjan Sabha. He approached Rahul in early 2010 to join the IYC. 'He sent me to meet Jitendra Singh but they wanted me to contest the IYC elections in Madhya Pradesh. I belong to the backward Patel caste there and have a following of about 10,000 voters,' he claimed. His community in Satna votes for the rival Bharatiya Janata Party and his inclusion in the IYC could tilt the balance, he added. Patel had been active in politics in that area for over seven years before he approached the IYC. He had been a trade union leader with the Bidi Mazdoor Sangh and had been booked by the state government for rioting. He was then a part of the CPM and had also fought elections for the mayor's post but lost. 'The SP had a few elected MLAs in the state and the CPM was not strong, so I joined the Party's youth wing to protect myself from harassment,' Patel said. He fought for the rights of the poor but the new IYC order has no place for him. 'The Youth Congress leaders want me to first enrol members and then contest the elections. This way, I will have to start all over again,' he complained. And with a criminal case against him, there was little chance of his nomination papers getting past FAME's scrutiny. The new format of inducting members into the IYC would pick up the likes of Szarita and Abdul but leave out many like Patel.

A note on the membership and election process of the IYC

Membership for the IYC is thrown open for thirty days in each state or union territory where elections are held. The membership forms are scrutinized, and codes are allotted to each and every panchayat in a state. In 2010, Tamil Nadu, for instance, saw nearly 20,000 panchayat-level elections for the state Youth Congress—a process that started in the month of January and ended in April.

Each panchayat elects a five-member committee. The posts of president and vice-president are thrown open to all contestants, including those for whom seats are reserved. The other three positions in the committee are reserved: one each for women, candidates from the Scheduled Castes and Scheduled Tribes, and those who belong to the OBCs or are minorities. At the gram-panchayat-level or the municipal-committee-level, the Youth Congress committee has five members. This is in the villages or the suburban areas. In the cities and larger towns where there are municipal corporations, the Youth Congress has a committee at every ward level which has ten members instead of five. These committees form the first tier of the Youth Congress structure. In every village or ward, there are hundreds of members who are the footsoldiers of the IYC, the foundation of the Congress's cadre-building exercise.

From bottom upwards, the new IYC is a four-tiered structure. The panchayat- and the municipal-ward-level committees all converge to elect the assembly-constituency-level committees which in turn form a Lok Sabha constituency-level committee. The Lok Sabha Youth Congress committees elect the PYC or the Pradesh (that is, state) Youth Congress. After the elections are complete at the state level all over the country, a new national-level IYC committee is formed. Here, unlike in the Congress, no one can predict who the president would be.

All members at every level elect an equal number of Youth Congress committee members and delegates. Only the delegates contest for the next level.

Building Brand Rahul

11 May 2011. Even though it was summer and the heat can get unbearable in the fields of western Uttar Pradesh that abut Delhi on the east, it wasn't yet hot. The sun had been out for barely a few minutes. Before the policemen who had been posted there—to prevent outsiders from reaching the twin villages of Bhatta and Parsaul in Greater Noida—could realize what was happening, Rahul Gandhi and his team managed to sneak past the cordons through a lesser-known route. They were at the site of a sit-in protest by farmers against the Mayawati government's land acquisition drive which had turned violent.

The farmers of the two villages believed that the rates offered to them by the government for taking their lands away—to hand them over to private builders to develop and sell—were unfair. They were being paid only a small part of what buyers were being charged by the private construction companies, which, apart from constructing the Yamuna Expressway passing through their lands, were building condominiums, malls and multiplexes. To add to the injustice of the state being in cahoots with the builders was the action of the state police force who had cracked down brutally on the farmers, leaving a number of them injured and a few homes ransacked. This had happened less than a week earlier. Unhappy with the land acquisition that was proceeding unhindered despite their pleas for better rates from the state government, the villagers were holding captive three lower-rung officials who had come there to conduct a pre-acquisition survey. They wanted to send a message to the state government: acquiring their lands would not come easy. A day after the government officials were illegally detained by the villagers, the state police came down on them heavily. A large posse of policemen descended on the villages and beat up several residents; according to some accounts, women and children were targeted. Newspaper reports said the police attack was so brutal that most of the men fled the villages. Many were ruthlessly thrashed and property was destroyed. It was against the backdrop of this violence that Rahul went to meet the farmers. In fact, people close to him claim that he had sought permission from the farmers, who were wary of politicians due to the incidents that preceded his visit, to join the sit-in protest. The Congress general secretary Digvijaya Singh had been to the villages to prepare the ground a day before Rahul's visit. This has been the pattern for the last few years: if you want to know what Rahul Gandhi's next move will be, just follow Digvijaya Singh.

Rahul sat in through the protest despite prohibitory orders from the administration. Later that night, he was in police custody—arrested for the first time in his life. During the course of a single day, he had managed to join a group of farmers otherwise hostile to politicians and had even got arrested like an ordinary citizen— demanding to be shown a proper arrest warrant—and whisked away by the local police despite his elite SPG cover. 'This was probably the first time that an SPG protectee was arrested. The SPG had never faced this situation before,' recalled a member of Rahul's team who had accompanied him to Greater Noida that day.

The police were all set to leave him at the UP–Delhi border and let him return to the capital. According to the associate who was with the Congress general secretary that day,

> Instead, he insisted on being shown the arrest papers. The police official heading the local police contingent that included jawans of the Rapid Action Force said that the papers were lying at the police station. On Mr Gandhi's insistence that he wanted to see the papers for his arrest, he was taken to the police station.

The day ended, but Rahul's association with the farmers did not. He followed up the visit by leading a delegation of the farmers to meet with the prime minister and demand a judicial inquiry into the violence unleashed by the state police on them. The visit came on the day that Mahendra Singh Tikait, the last big farmers' leader and founder of the Bharatiya Kisan Union, was cremated in his village in western UP. Tikait is best remembered as being a leader who could muster the support and participation of thousands of farmers in an agitation. In 1988, he had led several thousand farmers from all over north India to camp at Boat Club in the heart of Delhi to press for the acceptance of their demands. His message was simple: If the powers that run the country from Delhi didn't care, the peasants would lay siege to the capital and defecate on Rajpath, the road that leads from India Gate to the President's house. On 15 May, Rahul Gandhi put a batch of eight farmers from Bhatta and Parsaul villages face to face with the man occupying the highest seat of authority in the capital. As a career politician Rahul was sending a clear signal to the farmers that they would be heard in Delhi and that he, as someone from the political class which had ignored them all this while, would facilitate that. Tikait's message was to the powers that be in Delhi while Rahul's message was to the farmers.

The fact that farmers who were totally distrustful of politicians were ready to listen and willing to engage with Rahul was due to a combination of factors: he had been working hard with regard to those at the bottom of the pyramid and he had a plan in place. In addition to this he was another Gandhi. Even before he entered active electoral politics, Rahul Gandhi had enjoyed superstar status in India. Little was known about him, except that he belonged to the first family of Indian politics and was expected to succeed as the fourth prime minister from the Nehru–Gandhi clan. And since two of them—his grandmother Indira and father Rajiv—were victims of political assassination, he had grown up with rings of security around him. The kind of security that brings with it layers of secrecy.

Rahul Gandhi was a man with the kind of experience few politicians would have thought relevant: he had some training in business theory. His brief association with Monitor Group in London would have acquainted him with the theory of 'competitive advantage' put forth by the consultancy's chief founder, Michael Porter. You win either via a cost advantage or through a strategy of differentiation. The world's top brands always pick the latter—offering something that the others do not. These brands also insist on being brands in the truest sense: they pack together a consistent set of values that stay ever-relevant.

The happenings on 11 May 2011 and the days that followed are evidence of a strategy that Rahul and his advisers had honed to perfection and of a persona that had been created over years. When Rahul was taken into custody for the first time ever in his life, he had nearly perfected his stance of being on the side of the underdog. Yet, the aggressive manner in which he took on the Mayawati government caused some experienced older Congressmen to question the intentions of his advisers. When he led the farmers of the two villages to meet with the prime minister, Rahul submitted a long list of complaints on alleged police atrocities. He maintained that women had been raped in the villages and that his team had found a heap of ashes with human bones in them, suggesting that some missing villagers had probably been killed and their bodies burnt by the police. The statement led even veteran Congressman and Indira Gandhi's aide R.K. Dhawan, an old Nehru–Gandhi clan loyalist, to say that Rahul's advisers needed to be changed.

In a party where sycophancy is the minimum requirement for progress, to suggest that the leadership is being advised wrongly implies that the leadership is at fault. This is the only way for Congressmen to express their anguish when they think the leadership is not right. These occasions are rare, though, and the Congressmen in question run the risk of getting isolated or even fading into political oblivion. According to Arun Jaitley, leader of the Opposition in Rajya Sabha and former law minister in the NDA government, the problem lies with dynastic politics. 'In the event of a mistake, blame is always put on others and it is said the family was very angry,' he said. 'In this kind of a structure, a Gandhi can never commit a mistake, [he] can only be misled . . . A government cannot run like this,' he added, referring to the uneasy relationship between the Congress and the Gandhi family where the latter's actions are never questioned from within the Party.

Rahul had clearly gone overboard with his allegations which were hard to prove in the months to come. But, with his visit to Bhatta and Parsaul and the amount of coverage it garnered, he conveyed the impression that he stood with the farmers, even if they resorted to kidnapping state government officials to stall the process of their lands being taken away.

This event is illustrative of the way Rahul reaches out to the underprivileged and the manner in which the Congress rallies behind him to help sustain his pro-poor stance. The perception that everyone in the government and the Congress Party is attentive to his every utterance, of course, is a part of the package. The meeting with the prime minister resulted in the Centre announcing compensation for the farmers of Bhatta–Parsaul. When Rahul proposes, the Manmohan Singh government always obliges. Even the National Advisory Council headed by Sonia Gandhi does not enjoy such a privilege.

The journey—from visiting homes of farmers to leading a delegation of farmers to the prime minister's doorstep—had taken a few years. After he assumed charge as general secretary of the Party, Rahul began touring the rest of the country. Till then, he had largely confined himself to UP. Most of these tours were built around resurrecting the Party's youth wings, but the core purpose of the visits was to gain more and more experience in engaging with those who lived on the margins.

On Friday, 7 March 2008, the budget session was on and the two houses of Parliament would meet again in three days. While fellow parliamentarians were busy working on the politics that would play out at the centre of power, Rahul Gandhi decided to set up his political arena elsewhere. He set out to visit the most backward and ignored parts of the country. He wanted to familiarize himself with the lives of people from the 'other India' and establish links that he hoped would ultimately turn into bonds. A few hundred miles from New Delhi, the Amethi MP began a series of trips—news of which soon made headlines as 'Rahul's "discovery of India" tour'. His first stop was in Orissa's ore-rich but extremely backward tribal district, Kalahandi. This would be his first visit to Lanjigarh, but not the last. He interacted with a number of tribal men and women and assured them in small public meetings of his being their voice in New Delhi. He was as eager to know from them what they wanted from the government as he was to tell them that he was on their side. He spoke of the two Indias that were developing within the country—'one having access to education, health and employment and another that was lagging behind'. A few days later, he would refer to the two Indias in his budget speech in Parliament.

In Rahul's words, the UPA government had fulfilled its promises made to the *aam aadmi* during its four-year rule: the National Rural Employment Guarantee Act (NREGA), renamed after Mahatma Gandhi in 2010, and the Forest Rights Act were revolutionary legislations that would change the lives of the poor and the tribals. In his place any lesser-known Congressman could have been mistaken for a leader from one of the Left parties, given the manner in which he spoke to the people and the content of his speech. These were legislations for which the Left parties, too, claimed credit while supporting the UPA from outside. The Left, since it had begun to support the Congress-led UPA government, had successfully claimed credit for the government's pro-people tilt, especially for legislations like the NREGA, the Forest Rights Act and the Right to Information Act. In the series of visits that followed, Rahul would try to change that perception and wrest back the credit from the Left. Refusing to join Manmohan Singh's cabinet in both 2004 and 2009 allowed him the luxury of raising issues with ministries across the policy spectrum.

After the Left–UPA divorce in 2008, the UPA again returned to power. In its second run, the space vacated by the Left was occupied by Rahul and the NAC led by the Congress president. The day after Rahul's speech, a report in *The Hindu* said:

Expressing grave concern over the backwardness of the region, Mr Gandhi promised the tribals that he would continue to maintain the relationship that his grandmother and parents had established with them. He assured them that he would now be a part of their struggle for development in education, health care and employment.

The media was only too eager to cover Rahul's tour. *The Hindu* reported:

Addressing a Save Forest rally at Bhawanipatna, the district headquarters town of Kalahandi district, he said: '*Kalahandi ka, aur Adivasiyon ka Delhi mein ek sipahi hai; uska naam Rahul Gandhi hai*' (For Kalahandi and the tribals, there is a soldier in New Delhi; his name is Rahul Gandhi).'
    Earlier, he interacted with tribals at the Nangalbod gram panchayat in Nuapada district and the Ijurpa tribal hamlet in the Lanjigarh block of Kalahandi. At Ijurpa, the people belonging to the Dongria and Jharnia Kondh tribes opposing the setting up of an

alumina refinery in their locality sought Mr Gandhi's help. He promised them to take up the matter with the AICC president Sonia Gandhi.

More than two years later, during another session of Parliament—the first monsoon session of the 15th Lok Sabha with the Congress-led UPA back in the saddle—the lawmaker from Amethi once again left parliamentary proceedings behind for a meeting with tribal people and landowners at Kalahandi. There was a marked change in his appearance. He wore his trademark white kurta and pyjama attire with sneakers, but this time he also sported a beard. Addressing a congregation of tribal people in Lanjigarh, he said:

> You were fighting for your land and your faith and I said to you: 'Look, I live in Delhi. Your voice is being suppressed here but I am your soldier in Delhi.' But when I reached back and started making inquiries, I got to know that the voice of the tribal people is reaching Delhi and even outside India. I got to know that you were getting yourself heard far and that you were fighting for your rights. And, most importantly that you were fighting peacefully . . . I did what I could but this is your victory.

The victory he referred to was the minister for environment and forests Jairam Ramesh's rejection of the alumina mining project in the region. In 2011, Manmohan Singh moved Ramesh to head the crucial rural development ministry, another area of focus for the Congress in Rahul's plan. The Vedanta Mining Corporation, against which the local tribals had complained to Gandhi on his 2008 visit, was denied clearance for mining in the area despite protests from the Biju Janata Dal-led state government.

Rahul's beard and the mining project's rejection were not the only changes since the last visit. There was another marked difference. The helicopter in which Rahul travelled to address the public meeting did not land at the helipad built by the Vedanta Corporation. The corporation had extended the same courtesy to the Congress leader's team as it had in 2008, only, this time, the team had strict instructions not to take favours from Vedanta, a name synonymous in tribal minds with the exploitation of resources that were rightfully theirs. In the intervening months, Rahul had gradually learnt the importance of symbols. It was important not just to do things the right way but also to be seen as doing them the right way.

Surprise visits are part of the Rahul persona and much effort goes into projecting him as a serious man committed to the cause of poverty alleviation. In April 2010, he landed unannounced in Haryana's Mirchpur village, where a seventy-year-old Dalit man and his disabled daughter had been burnt alive by a group of Jats. Over fifteen Dalit houses had been set on fire. After he reached the village, accompanied by Congress leader Prithviraj Chavan, his SPG crew went up to the affected Dalit families posing as journalists. They said they wanted to speak to the families about the incident in private, and took some of them aside to the spot where Rahul was waiting; the idea was to avoid the hype that would be created by a visit made in the full glare of the media.

Such secrecy had worked in Rahul's favour earlier. When UP became the chief target of such visits, the Mayawati government had protested his actions furiously. But the Congress government in Haryana, led by Bhupinder Singh Hooda, did not dare display any irritation over his Mirchpur visit. The only Haryana government official present on his arrival was a *naib tehsildar* and that, too, by chance. The media was kept out, yet, the visit attracted more than enough media attention. The publicity machinery around Rahul ensures that the press is never denied details of such visits.

In the forty-five minutes that he spent at Mirchpur, Rahul heard out the victims. The Dalit families told him about their fears of being victimized further at the hands of the Jats. They wanted to be rehabilitated in some other village. Members of the dominant caste, they said, weren't allowing them to return to their homes. Rahul promised to inform the Congress president of their plight. Sure enough, Sonia pulled up Hooda for not reining in the perpetrators. 'Almost whenever he [Rahul] makes interventions, the outcome is favourable, and secondly, he makes calibrated interventions,' said Dilip Cherian, the Delhi-based image management executive who has handled a number of national election campaigns for political parties, including the Congress. 'I think he intervenes on subjects where he feels there is something to be done about them.' Every move is clearly well thought out. 'His team members are doing research all the time. The idea is only to expose him to issues that give him some traction,' Cherian added.

Delhi University professor and political analyst Mahesh Rangarajan reads a political statement in the issues Rahul takes up. Land, for example, is an important political issue, and an economic one as well. Best of all, it transcends caste and community affiliations. In his opinion, we can expect Rahul to replace Sonia Gandhi as the chief campaigner for Congress before the 2014 general election. It would mark a shift in the First

Family's core appeal: with the politics of sacrifice yielding to the politics of activism. Establishing public trust—that the shift would serve the country well—might not be as easy to achieve as putting together a plan. In itself, brand consistency (seen as espousing the same values and core issues, repeatedly) has served Rahul rather well so far. But, brand reliability (to be seen by the consumer, in this case the voter, as being able to deliver the goods he promises) is always harder to earn. His well-attended rallies have not resulted in proportionate electoral gains for the candidates for whom he campaigned. After the Janata Dal United and Bharatiya Janata Party combine swept the Bihar assembly elections in 2010, Jaitley took a dig at Rahul. 'The Congress should realize that politics is more than a series of photo-ops.'

***

Rahul Gandhi remained quite aloof from politics for many years. Then, he suddenly contested the Lok Sabha elections in 2004. He won comfortably from the family's pocket borough of Amethi in Uttar Pradesh, but he chose to take up neither a ministerial assignment in the first Congress-led coalition government nor a position in the Party. Despite pressure from all quarters within the Party, from leaders, tall and small, eager to associate with the next generation of the Congress, Rahul took his own time to decide what role he wanted for himself. His travels had actually begun with the 2004 Lok Sabha win. He first set out within his constituency, Amethi, stopping at frequent intervals and mingling with the villagers. Amethi and Rae Bareli, Sonia Gandhi's constituency, were relatively familiar territory for Rahul even then.

From the family's boroughs, he slowly expanded outwards into other parts of UP as the 2007 assembly elections drew closer. A roadshow in western UP as part of the election campaign took him to the Islamic seminary of Deoband. Interacting with the students there, he announced: 'I am blind to caste and religion. I see everyone as Hindustani . . . If one Hindustani tries to harm another, I promise I will come in between. Please remember that I am the grandson of Indira Gandhi.'

Amethi is a constituency that has always been contested, and mostly won, by someone from the Gandhi family or by a close confidant. The family has nurtured the constituency for decades, even during the periods when the Congress remained out of power at the Centre and in the state. But, campaigning and dealing with the voters of Amethi is not the same as dealing with voters in other parts of the country or even other parts of UP.

Three successive political movements—the rise of OBC politics, the Ayodhya temple movement and, later, the rise of Dalit politics—ensured that the Congress stayed out of power in the state. It was reduced to an insignificant position in most elections.

Rahul's remarks on the second day of his election campaign caused a stir. On 19 March 2007, he announced at Deoband, 'Had the Gandhi family been there in politics [at that time], Babri Masjid demolition would not have taken place.' It was the Congress that was in power at the Centre with P.V. Narasimha Rao as prime minister when the mosque was demolished by Hindu zealots at Ayodhya on 6 December 1992. 'My father said to my mother that he would stand in front of Babri Masjid if it would do any good. They would have had to kill him first,' Rahul told a gathering of listeners. The brief speech caused outrage even within his own party though Congressmen, as usual, were quick to defend it.

Analysts back in New Delhi dubbed it a display of political naivety and immaturity. On the same trip, at Bareilly, he said, 'Members of the Gandhi family have achieved goals they have initiated, like the freedom of the country and dividing Pakistan in two.' After years of staying away from politics and public life, Rahul was learning the art of speaking in public the hard way.

Unlike his sister, he was a slow learner and, to add to his worries, he has been more in the spotlight than any other Gandhi who had ventured into politics. Every word, in the age of twenty-four-hour news television, was picked up and scrutinized. Every nuance recorded and debated ad nauseam.

It was only after he was given charge of the youth organizations of the Party as general secretary in September 2007 that Rahul began to work to a plan. Within six months of taking charge of the youth organizations, he began traversing the length and breadth of India just as his father had after becoming prime minister in 1984, and his great-grandfather after returning to India. 'To me, the Orissa tour and all such tours are a journey in understanding and getting close to the people,' he told journalists in Bhubaneswar on the fourth day of his Orissa visit. When asked by a journalist on how long he planned to tour like this, his response was: 'It will continue for the rest of my life.'

Congress leaders say the travels that took him to all parts of the country laid the foundation for a more confident and more travelled future prime ministerial candidate from the Party. They also put him directly in touch with the professed target audience of the Congress—the common man. There were bloopers and mistakes on the way, as also criticism from the Opposition, but the travels seemed to have helped the Congress strike a chord with the voters. The returns were greater in 2009. Though the Congress tried to give Rahul the entire credit, it is probably true that it owed at least a part of its success to his travels. The apex body of the Congress—the CWC—passed a resolution in its first meeting after the 2009 results to congratulate Rahul on the Party's success. His campaign tour during the 2009 elections took him to more rallies than the prime minister and Sonia Gandhi put together. Rahul's aligning with the poorest of the poor seemed to have worked wonderfully as a political strategy as well as a learning experience.

Everywhere Rahul went, the media followed. An associate of his said the phrase 'Discovery of India' was a media coinage that Rahul and his team disliked but it stuck. Rahul was already travelling among the poor to understand how a large part of India lives. He felt the media were giving too much importance to the caste or the religion of the people whose homes he visited. At a press conference in Thiruvananthapuram, he told reporters:

> I see it as going to a human being's house and not a Dalit's house. I am going to a poor man's house,

whether he is a Dalit or belongs to a minority community or an upper caste. Dalit is your frame and not mine. While you see him as a Dalit, I see him as a poor person.

Rahul's primary aim was to understand what the poor go through and to know them better. 'All that I do is to understand what the poor people are faced with,' he said, adding that the only difference he saw between the poor and the rich was one of opportunity. At the Congress's 2010 plenary in New Delhi, it was clear that he wanted the Party to play the role of the provider of those opportunities to the poor which, when denied, kept them poor.

But, it was not by coincidence that the media were giving too much importance to the caste or class of people whom Rahul met during his travels. His visits to Bundelkhand and subsequent lobbying with the Central government earned the backward region a special package. He led a delegation to the prime minister to demand a relief package for handloom and powerloom weavers. And five days later, the finance minister, in his budget speech, announced a special bailout package for weavers. The media were quick to give him credit for the development even though Rahul's meeting with the prime minister came nearly a month after the minister of state for textiles,

Panabaka Lakshmi, announced to the weavers in her constituency that a package was on its way.

The weavers owed an estimated amount of Rs 3,400 crores to banks. Rahul suggested that the loan be waived. The delegation under Rahul—which included Congress general secretary Digvijaya Singh, Uttar Pradesh Congress Committee (UPCC) president Rita Bahuguna Joshi, and UP Congress leader Pramod Tiwari—submitted a three-page proposal to the prime minister. It read, 'The weavers, particularly in north India, are going through acute misery because of increase in prices of cotton yarn and silk yarn. Because of the policy of state governments, the powerloom and handloom sectors in Uttar Pradesh, Bihar and other states are in a very bad state.'

A few days later, the finance minister announced a Rs 3,000-crore package for the weavers' cooperative societies. Though Mukherjee did not specify the details of the allocation, Congressmen declared that the money was meant for a loan waiver. The Congress leadership had succeeded in projecting to the weavers that it was because of Rahul that their voice had been heard. Weavers form about 8 per cent of UP's population and due to the large concentration of their population in eastern UP, the Congress hoped that the waiver would influence voting patterns in the region.

When Rahul intervenes, the government acts. The Party goes all out to take note of and praise every little step that builds his image, or to put immediate corrective measures in place if necessary. Sycophancy isn't a trait Rahul encourages. But that doesn't discourage even the veterans in the Party from showering praises on the leader who is close to them neither in age nor in experience. Rahul, however, would rather be seen as one with the *aam aadmi*, whether it is through politically strategic moves like supporting the Aligarh farmers in their agitation against his rival Mayawati, or spontaneous decisions like travelling on a Mumbai local train during a visit to the country's financial capital.

On that visit, he sent both his security and the state administration into a tizzy by suddenly deciding to take a local train, the lifeline for lakhs of ordinary Mumbaikars. He waited patiently on the platform, waving to surprised commuters across the rail track on the opposite platform. Inside the train, he shared a seat with someone, talked to people, reached out to shake hands with them and even took a phone call straining to hear and be heard over the din in the compartment. And finally, when he got off the train, he left the station refusing to say a word to the mediapersons who had rushed through Mumbai traffic to catch up with him.

A talkative companion while on the train, he clammed up before the television microphones.

While his co-passengers were thrilled with the unexpected encounter, neither the Shiv Sena nor the Maharashtra Navnirman Sena (MNS) took kindly to the visit. After Rahul stopped at an ATM to draw money, MNS chief Raj Thackeray said, 'This is what they do at the Centre—take away money from Maharashtra.' A year later, when he took a local train from Dombivli to Dadar to escape traffic congestion, Thackeray did not lose the opportunity to take a dig at Rahul. 'I did not want to do any stunt. Unlike him, who had stopped to withdraw money from an ATM to buy tickets, I had money with me to buy my ticket,' he said. For the record, Thackeray was taking a Mumbai local after twenty-five years.

The surprise visit to Aligarh in August 2010 was one of the many such trademark visits Rahul has made in Uttar Pradesh. In Tappal, a village in Aligarh which had become the epicentre of the protests, he backed the farmers' demand for higher compensation for land acquired by the state government to build the 165-kilometre Noida–Agra Yamuna Expressway. The expressway is a project dear to Mayawati. He stood listening to the farmers in the heavy downpour and assured them that the Congress was on their side.

If there are outright confrontations, there are also subtle statements. In both cases, the purpose is often dual: to connect with the common man and, at the same time, ruffle the opponents. Despite the jibes, Rahul does not spare any chance to show himself as the ordinary man's leader—whether that means sitting in the stands rather than the VIP enclosure in the stadium during the Commonweath Games, or turning down the offer to spend the night in a plush suite at Yadavindra Gardens, Pinjore, opting, instead, for a regular room. Or, stopping on a busy Delhi road to help an accident victim and rush him to hospital.

With time and repeated efforts, Rahul's confidence has grown. Malcolm Gladwell's theory—if you want to shine, spend 10,000 hours honing your skills—seems to have worked for him. For many who have seen him in action, Brand Rahul now stands for a silent, serious man who wants to pull up the India that is lagging behind. He may be an outlier, but the question is whether the brand he has slowly built can outlast the contempt and the cynicism that twenty-first century India reserves for its politicians.

The Dalit Agenda

A small, weathered portrait of Babasaheb Bhimrao Ambedkar overlooks the entrance to Savita Saroj and Radhe Shyam Pasi's house. Their village, Hasua Survan, lies in the Jagdishpur block of a district that was created on 1 July 2010 and named Chhatrapati Shahuji Maharaj Nagar. The portrait hangs above the picture of the Hindu god Shiva. It has been there for years. It was there when Savita became the village *pradhan*, the chief, in 2000. It was there when the young, first-time MP of Amethi, Rahul Gandhi, came calling on 12 October 2004 and spent an entire afternoon in the Pasi-dominated village. He learnt some important lessons that day: One,

Ambedkar's portraits are common in this village with three out of every four homes belonging to a Dalit family. Two, Ambedkar's place in a Dalit home is a notch above that of a god.

'He sat with us and talked to the village women. There were more women than men and he refused to sit on the chair we brought him. He said he was there to know our problems and would know them better only if he sat on the ground like us,' recalled Savita, pointing to the white plastic chair on which Rahul Gandhi had declined to sit. Instead, he had squatted on the cement floor surrounded by the women of the village. She spoke about how 'Rahul bhaiyya' listened patiently and took notes. The government primary school in the village had had only one teacher for 200 students. It had four now. Radhe Shyam believes the improvement has something to do with the young MP's visit. But a lot more, he said, remains to be done. His children now go to private schools because the government school has classes only up to Class V. They have outgrown it and must cycle or walk to another school some distance away if they wish to study further. 'The village still doesn't have an *anganwadi* centre. [Successive] state governments have not done enough,' Radhe Shyam said in April 2010, on the eve of Rahul Gandhi's rally at Ambedkarnagar.

It was no ordinary rally and, in organizing it, Rahul was applying the lessons he had learned years ago at Radhe Shyam Pasi's village. The rally was held on 14 April, on Ambedkar Jayanti, in a town not only named after the Dalit icon but also considered the UP Chief Minister Mayawati's bastion. It had flagged off ten chariots which fanned out into Uttar Pradesh to take on her might and break the success formula of the Bahujan Samaj Party (BSP). The idea was to replace that with the Congress's own formula: To rule UP, play the Ambedkar card and divide the Dalit vote.

The visit to the Pasi village had happened a long time ago, when Rahul was just starting out as a politician, a few months after he fought and won the Lok Sabha election of 2004. This was long before the Opposition parties accused him of visiting Dalit homes for political gain (only to ape him later). It was long before the Congress began working on regaining power in UP in 2012. But it was because of visits like these that the Congress eventually found the courage to take on the BSP.

The rally was a direct affront to the BSP and its politics, showcasing the Congress intention to overthrow it. 'We plan to oust Mayawati from her seat of power in the next assembly elections. We plan to make the Dalits and all the other communities in the state aware of her misrule and to save the state from a tyrant,' said Rita Bahuguna Joshi, UP Congress chief, revealing for the first time her leader's grand plan to wrest power in the state. 'Corruption and anarchy have halted the development of UP. No wonder Mayawati is uncomfortable with our *rath yatra*,' she added.

In the run-up to the rath yatras, there was tension between the workers of the two parties. They almost fought over the placement of posters and billboards in the district. An early set of posters for Rahul's 14 April rally—which featured Congress leaders prominently, but not Ambedkar—was criticized by the BSP. The second set of posters from the Congress organizers included not only Ambedkar but also the Party's long-standing Dalit face, Babu Jagjivan Ram. Seniors leaders hurled accusations at each other. The state president of the BSP and state cooperative minister Swami Prasad Maurya, said: 'The people of the country are aware of the Congress conspiracy to keep them ignorant and poor. So, such rath yatras don't bother us.' Despite its nonchalance, the BSP launched a counter agitation. Maurya described it as 'a movement across the state to expose the Congress and tell the people how the Centre is using the CBI and the income tax department to victimize Behenji'.

While the Congress launched a drive to connect with the Dalits, the BSP launched a state-wide campaign against Sonia Gandhi's dream legislation, the Women's Reservation Bill. Party leaders went around telling the BSP's core constituents—the Dalits—that the bill would harm their interests. In July 2010, Mayawati struck back at Rahul Gandhi for daring to begin his battle to oust her in Ambedkarnagar. She carved out a new district that included parts of Rahul's and his mother's constituencies, Amethi and Rae Bareli, and christened it Chhatrapati Shahuji Maharaj Nagar.

The Congress hopes that as the 2012 assembly elections approach it would have done enough to ensure that Dalits weren't just Dalits anymore—that they would be split into groups—and that not all groups would be equally committed followers of the BSP. Take the example of Ram Tirath Pasi, a small-time but committed politician in Jagdishpur. At the Public Works Department's *dak* bungalow at the block headquarters, he spends time listening to the woes of fellow Dalits. Meeting people, discussing their problems and attempting to solve them has been a way of life for Ram Tirath since 1978 when, as a young undergraduate at the Ganpat Sai Degree College, he had gone to Pratapgarh to listen to Mayawati's mentor Kanshi Ram, then the BSP chief. Kanshi Ram has spoken of a Dalit revolution. After graduation, Ram Tirath joined Kanshi Ram first as part of his social outfit, the Dalit Shoshit Samaj Sangharsh Samiti, and later as a full-time activist of the All India Backward and Minority Communities Employees' Federation.

It was from the Jagdishpur assembly constituency in 1984 that a young Ram Tirath—not even thirty then—had contested on the ticket of the newly formed BSP. He lost, but he managed to get over five thousand votes. Politics became a part of his life. While Kanshi Ram was still alive but ailing, and as Mayawati slowly took control of the Party, Ram Tirath moved out forever. He said, 'The BSP today is not the BSP I was part of. There is unrest among the Dalits over Mayawati's approach to politics. Her formula of building a *sarvjan samaj* is obviously at the cost of the Bahujan Samaj.' Kanshi Ram referred to the Dalits and the downtrodden as the '*bahujan samaj*' because their numbers exceeded the population of the upper castes. He looked to the consolidation of the oppressed to wrest power for the Dalits. Mayawati, however, realized that Dalit votes alone were not enough. During the 2007 assembly elections, she adopted the slogan of 'sarvjan samaj' and roped in the Brahmins and the Muslims to get the clear majority she needed to become chief minister of UP. Ram Tirath insists that it is the Dalits who have brought Mayawati to power each time she won, while it is the Brahmins—far fewer in number—who have been responsible for the woes of the Dalits. 'How can this equation ever make sense to a poor, marginalized Dalit?' he asks.

As Ram Tirath delved deeper into the reasons for his disenchantment with Mayawati's politics, it emerged that Mayawati had been partial to her own caste, the Jatavs or the Chamars, he said. 'We did the hard work but the benefits went to others. When Mayawati filled the backlog of vacancies left behind by the Congress and the BJP governments, she filled them with Jatav candidates.' Ram Tirath had no proof of his allegation, but in politics, perception is enough to tilt the scales. Statistics and proof are for analysts, not voters.

One out of every five people in UP is a Dalit. Besides being of Mayawati's caste, Chamars or Jatavs form the biggest chunk of UP's Scheduled Caste population: 56.3 per cent according to the 2001 census. The Pasis, at 16 per cent, are the second largest group of Dalits in the state. Together with the Dhobi, the Kori and the Balmiki, the two castes form the bulk of UP's Dalit population—87.5 per cent, to be precise.

Among the Dalits, too, caste matters. When the Congress's P.L. Punia won the Lok Sabha seat in 2009

from Barabanki, newspapers widely reported that the
BSP chief had spent more than half an hour of a meeting
held to assess the Lok Sabha results talking about Punia.
'I wonder if you know that Punia is not a Chamar. He is
a Dhanuk from Haryana,' Mayawati is said to have told
her party leaders. A former bureaucrat, Punia had been
Mayawati's principal secretary during her earlier stints
as chief minister in 1995, 1997 and 2002. Differences
developed between the two at the time of the Taj
Corridor case. Taj Corridor was a project to upgrade
tourist facilities near the Taj Mahal in which Mayawati's
government was charged with corruption. Rahul Gandhi
and his advisers on UP pulled off a coup of sorts by
getting Punia on their side. The latter had worked closely
with Kanshi Ram and Mayawati. Rather too closely for
Mayawati's comfort. He moved from being Mayawati's
trusted lieutenant to becoming a crucial player in Rahul
Gandhi's 2012 assembly election plans in UP. On 14 April
2010, he led one of the ten yatras flagged off by Rahul
through Dalit-dominated areas.

In Punia's words:

Our agenda is clear: To talk about the Congress's long-
standing commitment to the Dalits. We will expose
the BSP's nefarious plots in caste politics, and its

corruption during different stints. In the twenty-one years since the state last had a Congress government in power, things have gone bad. We will talk about this and expose Mayawati's rule. We are also going to talk about the Congress's contribution to the progress of the nation—economic development, the IT and telecom revolutions.

Punia thinks he was largely responsible for building up Mayawati's image of an able administrator. 'People say her first three stints as chief minister were good because governance was my responsibility,' he said in a self-congratulatory tone.

Towards the end of 2010, the UPA government appointed Punia chairman of the National Commission for Scheduled Castes (NCSC). He assumed the role of a man on a mission. He proclaimed he was fighting with all his might to eradicate untouchability. Only, a large part of that might has been directed at catalyzing the process of making the Congress the principal challenger to Mayawati in the UP assembly elections of 2012.

Punia had taken it upon himself to educate the Dalits of the state about their rights and also about the policies of the Congress-led UPA government at the Centre. As chairman of the NCSC, he got the commission to organize awareness camps in every district of Uttar Pradesh where he met the Dalits and informed them about the schemes launched by the Centre and the safeguards provided for them in the Constitution. But more interestingly, through these awareness programmes, Punia also assessed the mood of the Dalit votes in the state and reported back to the Party high command. At the end of the exercise, he submitted reports to his party about its prospects in the coming elections.

Between December 2010 and February 2011, the commission conducted eighteen awareness camps in UP—one each at all the divisional headquarters, each division comprising a few districts. The commission's report on the outcome stated that the local Congress had lost an opportunity by not using these camps to its advantage. 'Schedule for the meetings was drawn in advance and intimation sent to the AICC general secretary/secretary-in-charge, UP Congress Committee president, all MPs, MLAs and important Congress leaders,' Punia said in the report, lamenting the fact that Congress leaders and workers had largely stayed away from the awareness camps.

The report spoke of a strong 'anti-Mayawati' sentiment in the state 'which the Congress must capitalize on. Very large number of cases of Dalit atrocities came which were not registered with the police and in most cases of atrocities BSP functionaries and leaders were the main culprits.' When asked, Punia showed no qualms about using the commission's machinery to further the interests of the party he belonged to. Recounting his meeting with the Gandhis, Punia said, 'I submitted the report personally to madam (Sonia Gandhi) and Rahulji. He said, "Continue aggressively with your effort and let me know if you need my help, I am there."'

To add to the BSP government's woes, Punia enjoys the privilege of being a state guest when he visits the state because as NCSC chairman he is accorded the rank of a cabinet minister. In fact, the Mayawati government decided to amend the UP State Guest Rules, 1961, under which Punia enjoys guest status. Mayawati makes no bones about her dislike of Punia, and he makes no effort either to hide his contempt for her. Punia claimed that she has been gunning for him ever since they fell out.

She put eighteen of her ministers on the job to make sure that I did not win the election, but I did. The ministers were from all castes and religions. She wanted to influence the voters of Barabanki on the basis of caste and religion, yet I won by 1.68 lakh votes, and the BSP candidate was relegated to the third place.

Punia has accused the Mayawati government of misusing central funds meant for Dalit welfare, and the NCSC has issued notices. 'When I was in the government, I used to look after the Dalit agenda. The villages were never starved of funds,' he said. In his assessment, voters in UP were moving towards the Congress again but there was much to be done. 'The Party has to work very systematically and project itself as a viable alternative that is fit to win in all constituencies,' he continued, adding: 'If the Congress projects a Dalit leader, that will quicken the process of weaning Dalits away [from the BSP].' He didn't need to say which Dalit leader he had in mind.

There was already a sense of unrest among the Dalits in the state due to Mayawati's style of governance. Combine that with Rahul Gandhi's visits to Dalit homes, and the Congress might just come up with a winning formula, said R.K. Chaudhary, a Pasi leader and long-time associate of Kanshi Ram. Chaudhary was once a minister in Mayawati's cabinet, but was thrown out of the BSP in 2001. 'When a leader goes to the people, he gains,' Chaudhary said. He felt that the growing influence of Brahmins in the BSP had forced the Dalits to rethink their support of Mayawati and, with the right moves, the Congress might just be able to forge a new and effective alliance. Though Chaudhary did not join the Congress, Rahul got the Party to extend support to his candidature from Mohanlalganj during the 2009 elections. The seat went to the Samajwadi Party (SP), but the foundation was laid for an alliance between the Pasis and the Congress.

Rahul Gandhi's Dalit agenda is to convert the anti-incumbency sentiment against Mayawati, whatever its extent, into votes for the Congress. His visits to Dalit homes were not merely educational trips as the Opposition mocked in the beginning. Consider this: On 23 September 2009, Rahul was on a less publicized visit to the state. He visited the Ram Nagar area in Barabanki district, and then Chutkaideh village in Shravasti district to spend the night in the house of a Dalit *gram pradhan*, a Pasi. 'For one used to comforts, the thirty-nine-year-old son of Congress president Sonia Gandhi even bathed in the open, drawing water from a hand-operated water pump,' an agency report in a newspaper proclaimed two days later. 'It was incredible. We rarely get to see the face of the local MLA (legislator) whom we have elected. Therefore, a visit by someone like Rahul Gandhi will always remain etched in our memories,' said Chedda

Pasi, son of the Rampur–Deogan village head. The report quoted him as saying that the last VIP to visit the village, in 1997, was Arif Mohammed Khan, a one-time associate of Rahul's father who joined the BSP after his deep disillusionment with the Congress. 'Gandhi's journey, aimed at understanding the way the poor live across India, was the most significant trip by the Congress MP to any place outside of Amethi and Rae Bareli,' wrote journalist Sharat Pradhan, on 1 October 2009, for the India Abroad News Service.

It is not a matter of mere coincidence, though, that Rahul Gandhi's surprise overnight stays with Dalits often took place in non-Jatav homes. The Congress realizes that if at all it can win Dalit votes, it will not be those of the Jatavs. On 17 May 2008, Rahul took the residents of Banpurwa village by surprise when he landed at the meeting of a women's self-help group that provides microfinance. He chatted with the women for a long time and then asked one of them, Rekha Pasi, to serve him food at her home. In January 2009, when he had accompanied the then-British Foreign Secretary David Miliband to a Dalit village in Amethi, he had stayed at the house of Shivkumari, a Kori.

As Rahul's stays at Dalit homes virtually became a trend, other Congress leaders decided to follow suit. On

2 October 2009, leaders of the UP Congress decided to mark Gandhi Jayanti by 'doing a Rahul'. They set out to spend a night in a Dalit's home. But, unlike Rahul, some of these party workers landed at Dalit homes with personal cooks, their own plates, pedestal fans, mosquito nets and mattresses. The message they sent out wasn't quite in sync with what Rahul intended to convey. The sole element of similarity was that these Congressmen also spent the night at non-Jatav houses. In the end, it was no surprise that these night visits by the state leaders, which had been meant to be a once-a-month affair, ended with the first one. But Rahul's forays into Dalit homes continued, though he has repeatedly asserted that it is the poor he visits and not Dalits. At a meeting of the NSUI at Jawaharlal Nehru University on 30 September 2009, he repeated that assertion. The next month, addressing the media in Thiruvananthapuram, he said: 'I ask my office to arrange for my visit to a poor man's home in the poorest village. You see him as a Dalit. I see him as a poor person.'

On 19 January 2010, on a visit to Madhya Pradesh for the IYC membership drive, he told reporters in Bhopal: 'The media talks only about my visits to the houses of Dalits and chooses to ignore the other places where I go.' Denials of there being a larger agenda behind these visits are frequent, but the pattern in these visits is too obvious to ignore.

Mayawati's exasperation clearly grew as the pattern became obvious. In April 2008, she said at a press conference that Rahul Gandhi uses special soap to bathe after visiting Dalit homes. Days later, at another press conference, Rahul laughed as he stood up and asked journalists: 'Look at me. Do I look like I use special soap?' The spontaneity of the act from an otherwise-reserved man sent the journalists into raptures. They knew that the Mayawati–Rahul–Dalit soap was just beginning to get exciting.

Mission 2012 Recast

Rahul Gandhi's reluctance to enter politics was outweighed only by his eagerness to see the Congress regain its old glory in the Hindi belt. As soon as he contested his first Lok Sabha election, his eyes were set on reviving the Congress's fortunes in Uttar Pradesh. Rahul's logic, which he often shared with his team, is simple and irrefutable: The three states of Uttar Pradesh, Bihar and Madhya Pradesh together send nearly 150 MPs to the Lok Sabha, and capturing these three political arenas would ensure that the grand old party could once again come to power, on its own, at the Centre.

'I live in Delhi but my heart is in UP,' he told a gathering at a public meeting he was addressing in western UP. That he was a fourth-generation parliamentarian from UP only helped firm up Rahul's resolve.

In January 2006, when he made that unscheduled speech at the Congress Hyderabad plenary, Rahul made it clear that, once he took charge of things Congress leaders would have to work hard. It was no use, he said, blaming casteist or communal parties for the Congress's plummeting fortunes in the region: 'We have failed to live up to people's expectations, we have stopped fighting for their causes and we have lost the ability to link the Party organization with our workers and people.' Between 2006 and the Lok Sabha polls in 2009, Rahul's remarks and his extensive touring of the state often drew cynical responses from various quarters. Sometimes, they originated from within his own party, though in hushed tones. The 2009 Lok Sabha election, however, was a turning point. From being a party that was barely a contender, having won just nine seats in the 2004 Lok Sabha polls, the Congress jumped to a figure of twenty-one seats, making it the second largest seat clincher, just behind Mulayam Singh Yadav's Samajwadi Party. In fact, the Congress's gains in the 2009 elections spurred Mayawati to focus on wooing voters from among the Dalits and the Muslims even if it came at the cost of the Brahmins.

Soon after the formation of the 15th Lok Sabha, with great gusto the Congress launched its Mission 2012. The Party's aspiration was to form a government in UP by winning the 2012 assembly polls or at least to make a comeback in the state's politics from its current position of little relevance. In the 2007 assembly polls, Mayawati had used a combination of Brahmin and Dalit votes to reach a majority in the state assembly. Rahul Gandhi hoped to re-jig her formula to regain the Congress's winning combination in the late 1980s: Brahmins, Muslims and Dalits. The Party, just like the BSP, hoped to select candidates for the 2012 polls as early as the start of summer 2011.

After the Congress suffered heavy losses in Bihar, however, the Party cadres which had been working on the grand plan to wrest UP from Mayawati seemed to lose direction. In terms of votes and seats, the Bihar assembly elections in 2010 brought negative returns and loads of embarrassment for the Congress Party and its former allies—Lalu Prasad's Rashtriya Janata Dal (RJD) and Ram Vilas Paswan's Lok Janshakti Party (LJP)—which had fought the election together as an alliance in an attempt to oust the Nitish Kumar government. But, not only did Nitish Kumar's Janata Dal United (JD-U)–Bharatiya Janata Party combine return to power, it also came back with a clearer mandate. The challengers—Lalu and Paswan, and the Congress—who had contested all 243 seats and were hoping to play kingmaker, fared worse than they had in the previous round.

The negative returns in terms of votes and seats were partially offset by the valuable lessons that the losers picked up from this election. The first lesson was that anti-incumbency could no longer be taken for granted. The voters showed that, if the incumbent government was better than the alternative that the challengers were offering, they would not vote it out just for the sake of a change. Change, for the better, is what the electorate had sought in the previous assembly election when it got rid of the Lalu–Rabri rule. Nitish Kumar had formed his government on the promise of that change and, once in the saddle, he actually did set out to change things.

In the five years of his first regime, the Bihar government gave the state a semblance of governance. At the time of the 2010 assembly polls, when the voters set out to elect a new government, the state did not have enough power or much industry, but it certainly was not Lalu-land anymore. Law and order was restored to a very large extent. Not only were there better roads now, which had become non-existent during the fifteen years of Lalu's regime, one could actually move freely on them. The road from Patna, the state capital, to Siwan—a small town in western Bihar that had become infamous for crime—is a mere 150 kilometres. While covering the assembly elections in 2010, one of the authors travelled the stretch. It took a little over two hours to drive from Siwan to Patna. It would have taken up to eight hours about ten years earlier, according to Raj Kumar, a taxi driver and resident of Patna. 'No one would take the road after 3 p.m.,' he said, to underline the extent of lawlessness that prevailed under the stewardship of Lalu Prasad Yadav and, later, his wife Rabri Devi. The manager of the hotel where we put up for the night narrated an incident of kidnapping that he had witnessed right outside his office about seven years ago. Once famous as the district to which India's first president Dr Rajendra Prasad belonged, Siwan had become infamous during Lalu's time due to Mohammed Shahabuddin, a criminal and MP from his party. Shahabuddin, booked in multiple cases of murder and other heinous crimes, has been serving a prison sentence since 2007. The manager spoke of how—though the staff still locked the iron gates after midnight—the hotel now welcomed guests even at night.

Sending children to school was incentivized during Nitish's rule through free bicycles and uniforms, and enrolments went up. Through most of the five-year period, the state's economic growth was higher than the national average. Even the Gujarat chief minister and BJP leader Narendra Modi, who had been kept out of the campaign by Nitish, held a press conference in Ahmedabad to congratulate him, dubbing the 2010 victory 'a win for development and governance'.

When Rahul descended on the scene during the campaign for the Bihar polls in the winter of 2010, he promised a better state of affairs. He said at a rally in Manjhi near Chhapra:

We [the UPA] worked for Backwards and Dalits, and on the issue of poverty, and you brought us back to power in 2009. We have brought in the world's largest employment programme, which ensures 100 days' employment. But here, people don't get more than 30 days. More money [than what is sent to other states] is sent to Bihar for the Indira Awaas Yojana . . . The poor don't get that money, the rich do.

The crowd clapped. In Bihar, the poor are pitched against the poorer, and Rahul Gandhi played the role of the messiah of the poorest. In his rallies, Nitish compared his Bihar with that of Lalu. But Rahul Gandhi wanted

Biharis to compare their state with Delhi or Mumbai. In any case, his presence in the campaign seemed to have transformed the Congress from being a fence-sitter to something of a player. The Congress jumped into the battle with a promise of development that would out-develop Nitish. The results, however, showed that after fifteen years of Lalu's rule and promises, the people of Bihar were content to go with Nitish Kumar who had proven he was better than his predecessor.

When the first list of Congress candidates appeared in New Delhi, Rahul's fingerprints were clearly visible on it. Of the 243 candidates fielded—with the Party contesting all the seats after a long time—118 were below the age of forty (one-third were under thirty-five). Also, forty-seven Congress tickets went to Muslims, who constitute 16.5 per cent of the state population and are said to hold sway in a quarter of the seats. 'The idea was to give tickets to those who could be recognized as Congress representatives even after the elections, whether they won or lost,' revealed a source privy to the strategy formulated by Rahul Gandhi's team. 'At this stage, winning a large number of seats is not the goal. The real aim is to prove to sceptics that the Congress can go it alone. The BJP will obviously try to run it down as a Congress failure, but the idea here is to convince the average Congressman in Bihar that the Party will not make opportunistic alliances at his cost,' he added.

The Congress was hopeful of doing better than it had the previous time. Congress leaders on the campaign trail spoke of a Rahul wave in the state. In the more private setting of an airport lounge, a Congress chief minister told one of the authors that the Party hoped to more than double its earlier tally. The Congress closely watched the BJP's performance and hoped to drive a wedge between the JD-U and the BJP if the electoral arithmetic gave it a chance. 'If we can cross the thirty-seat mark, who knows, we might end up in government with Nitish Kumar,' the chief minister said. Only, the Party fell miserably short of its own expectations while the NDA emerged stronger.

The only electoral gain for the Congress was the marginalization of its troublesome former allies Lalu and Paswan. As long as these two remain relevant in Bihar politics, the Party cannot achieve Rahul Gandhi's dream of an all-powerful Congress at the Centre.

The Congress's chief opponent at the Centre and one of the principal competitors in the Hindi belt, the BJP, had fared better than it had in the last Bihar election by keeping Hindutva out of the election rhetoric and playing junior partner to the JD-U. This tactic would automatically erode, to some extent, the secular platform from which the Congress had been able to wrest back power from a non-secular BJP-led alliance. The BJP could replace the Congress's rhetoric of the secular/non-secular axis by employing its Bihar strategy. If the Mandal–mandir phase of electoral politics was coming to an end, then clearly there were opportunities as well as threats for the Congress.

The Bihar election showed that Rahul could draw crowds to his public meetings but the votes would come only if the Congress put up strong candidates. Paradropping the Party's youth face did not work—not on polling day. Yet, the Party may have made some gains in the election: Lalu could no longer claim that the MY (Muslim–Yadav) combination 'is my vote bank'. Nor could Paswan claim to command Dalit votes. It is not as if caste had disappeared with that election. Nitish Kumar had managed to create new constituencies for himself through positive discrimination during his tenure. He worked for women, Extremely Backward Castes and Mahadalits (all Dalit castes in Bihar except Paswans), and was able to wean voters away from vote banks that were traditionally supposed to belong to others.

The Congress finished at the bottom of the tally. In its campaign, it had set out to offer a post-Nitish era.

It had tried to sell to the people of Bihar the idea that the Party could be an improvement on what Nitish's rule had to offer, but without anything to show for it on ground. As a result, it put up its worst show ever in the state. It is naive, however, to suggest that the Congress applied the same formula to the Bihar 2010 polls that it planned to use in UP for 2012. Clearly, in Bihar, the Party had invested in the future, giving out nearly half its tickets to candidates below the age of forty. But the Party needs to realize that if it wants a future in the state, it will have to start by tackling its present situation. Rahul cannot be the Party's face in a state election unless he is running for chief minister. The Congress had no local face in the 2010 Bihar elections. As soon as the results started pouring in, the Congress went on the back foot to defend its leadership. General secretary in charge of the state, Mukul Wasnik, in his first media comments after the results, was more concerned about profusely thanking the Party president and Rahul for addressing rallies in Bihar than admitting that the central leadership could not fill in for a weak or non-existent state leadership.

When asked if the Bihar debacle meant the failure of Rahul's strategy, Congress general secretary Digvijaya Singh said:

Please do not connect Rahul Gandhi with what happened in Bihar. We have not done well in the state for ten–fifteen years, and that is because we have been aligning with Lalu Yadav. We have got the disadvantage of being on the wrong side. The fact remains that we got four seats in the 2004 Lok Sabha, and this came down to two seats in 2009. In the assembly, we got nine seats in 2004 and this has come down to four, so we have not really done worse over the past few years, but yes, we have not been able to gain.

Digvijaya Singh, who is in charge of UP for the Party, denied that the Congress had adopted a go-slow policy on Mission 2012, though he did admit to a tactical shift in the plan. The ten rath yatras that Rahul had flagged off on 14 April 2010 (B.R. Ambedkar's birthday) from Ambedkarnagar were to enter their second phase on 2 October 2010 (Mahatma Gandhi's birthday), and end on 10 November at Anand Bhavan (Nehru's house) in Allahabad, four days before Nehru's birthday. The plan was unceremoniously dropped after the poor show by Congress in Bihar. 'We have one full year. We will begin the second phase soon. The approach has been changed. We will go in for an agitational approach in every assembly segment,' Digvijaya Singh said in an interview to one of the authors.

Bihar ensured that the Party shifted its focus from micromanaging UP from the Centre to moving the preparations for the 2012 elections to the state capital. Acting on rumours that Chief Minister Mayawati could advance the election by a few months, the Congress got into the act of finalizing its candidates by mid-2011. The meeting of the Central Screening Committee of the AICC was moved to Lucknow from Delhi, after three decades, to shortlist candidates for UP's 403 seats. For a party hoping to return to power at the Centre on the basis of its performance in the states, decentralization seemed like a natural move. Except that it didn't come naturally to the Congress.

When Rahul made his first trip to the backward region of Bundelkhand, he approached Professor Sudha Pai of the Centre for Political Studies, Jawaharlal Nehru University, and author of *Dalit Assertion and the Unfinished Revolution: The BSP in Uttar Pradesh*, for a meeting to understand UP better. 'When he met me, he had already read my books. He was here to discuss, not to be spoon-fed,' Pai recalled. A close Rahul Gandhi observer since then, she accompanied him to a Congress meeting in Chitrakoot, Bundelkhand, along with a group of political scientists.

She wrote in the *Indian Express* after Rahul's grand rally in 2010 at Mayawati's citadel, Ambedkarnagar:

Will the massive mobilisation by the Congress Party under Gandhi make his 'Mission 2012' of capturing power in the next state assembly election successful? While it is early days yet, the Congress faces a Herculean task with enormous challenges from within and outside. UP is a big state, and obtaining a majority requires performing well beyond family strongholds. Organisational hurdles such as building strong local leadership and machinery across the state, internal elections, removing factionalism, finding winnable candidates with clean records, have yet to be resolved. Despite the discourse on development, Dalit/OBC issues retain importance and the BSP's success in the by-elections last year indicate that Mayawati's grip over her Dalit–Bahujan constituency remains strong, while the SP remains a contender with its vote-percentage remaining intact in 2007. What is clear is the emergence of a highly competitive, no-holds-barred political rivalry in the run-up to the next election, between the Congress attempting to regain lost ground as a broad-based party, and the BSP attempting to consolidate its position as a party of disadvantaged sections with a Dalit core.

A single paragraph of the political scientist's observations lists out several constraints that the Congress must overcome to gain UP, failing which, the assembly election will remain merely an interesting electoral fight. For Rahul, however, it could stretch further the long road to the Congress's dream of forming a government on its own at the Centre. The massive exercise of getting ten *chetna* yatras—that is, awareness marches—to travel through different places almost flopped. 'If at all, the marches have allowed Mayawati's followers to consolidate the BSP's position wherever the marches went. After a Congress yatra passes through an area, the BSP cadres take the opportunity to talk about their party and about Mayawati's rule to her vote bank. They tell the people that the Congress is conspiring to dislodge Maya from her position and that only leads to the consolidation of votes in her favour,' said a journalist working with a national Hindi news channel in Lucknow.

After he travelled to the villages of Bhatta and Parsaul in Greater Noida to join the farmers in their agitation against the government in May 2011, Rahul launched a four-day *padyatra*, a march on foot, through the villages along the Yamuna Expressway project. The journey, covered extensively in the media, gave a boost to Rahul's desire to make the Congress seem like the principal challenger to Mayawati's regime. It ended with a massive meeting of farmers in Aligarh, where the farmers' agitation against land acquisition for the project had begun in 2010. 'When a rich man sells his house, he gets the market rate. When a poor man asks for the market rate, he gets bullets. This is what I have understood after walking among you for four days,' Rahul told a gathering of farmers. 'That is why I walked,' he told a young farmer in the gathering who asked Rahul why he had walked when he had cars at his disposal.

'Your government only needs to come here and talk to you. A solution can be found, the government just needs to change its intention a bit. We can give you a good law but we can't change the intention of your [state] government,' he told another group of farmers at one of the several meetings he held during his march. The state government's land acquisition drive in western UP had left the peasants there feeling wronged. Rahul, after a failed attempt at targeting Mayawati through the chetna yatras of the Congress, found a good opportunity to use the ire against the BSP government and its chief.

In November 2011, Rahul reinitiated the Congress's bid for UP. Not only was the new campaign an admission that the Party had failed to convert the awareness campaign he launched in April 2010 into a wave, it was also a step backwards in his politics: Rahul chose to play the dynasty card. The time and the place for his rally to launch the Congress into election mode were carefully chosen. It was on 14 November 2011, the 122nd birth anniversary of his great-grandfather and India's first prime minister, Jawaharlal Nehru, at Phulpur near Allahabad. Phulpur was Nehru's political bastion from where he had won the first Lok Sabha election. Rahul launched a more aggressive-than-ever tirade against the Mayawati government and Mulayam Singh Yadav's Samajwadi Party.

The Party's posters and banners shouted out Rahul's Nehru connection—with the slogan '*Nehruji ko yaad karenge, Rahulji ke saath challenge* (We will remember Nehru, and go with Rahul)'—all over Allahabad. Hardened by his experience in politics, Rahul himself was more measured in invoking the Nehru–Gandhi dynasty, unlike in 2007, when he had infamously taken credit for belonging to the family that split Pakistan. 'At one time, Nehruji was the MP here, today mafiamen are the MPs here. There has been a lot of change in UP but no development,' he said, subtly reminding those gathered there of the Nehru connection.

The last time around, in Ambedkarnagar, on the BSP founder Kanshi Ram's birthday, there had been no mention of the dynasty. Instead, Rahul had spoken of moving on from the casteist and communal politics that was keeping UP backward. Both the Party and its emerging leader seemed to have taken a few steps backwards this time. Hitting out at the top leaders of the SP and the BSP, he said:

I have been in politics for seven years and I have been touring all of India and UP. In these tours, you have taught me the most. The poor in UP taught me that if a leader does not go to people's homes, eat with them and see them toil, he will not understand poverty. Until a leader drinks the dirty water from wells in their homes and falls ill, he will not understand anything about poverty. And, until a leader understands poverty in the homes of the poor, he will never be angry at the atrocities against the poor in the state. There was probably a time when Mayawatiji and Mulayam Singh Yadavji had this anger in them. Today, it has died in them and they are running after power.

Turning on the heat, he continued, 'How long will you continue to beg in Maharashtra or work as labourers in Punjab? When are you going to change the government here? Tell me right now. I want a reply. Let all of us join hands to bring about the change.' He added: 'Sometimes I think I should come to Lucknow to fight for you myself.' The remark drew a round of protests from the Opposition that dubbed it insensitive to the people of UP. The mild suggestion that he might even run for the top post of the chief minister was a tad late. A few days later, he launched his mass contact programme from Barabanki district, once again accusing the Mayawati government of siphoning off central funds meant for the poor. Rahul asserted that, if the state's voters elected a Congress government in 2012, UP would be among India's top states in five years.

In the meanwhile, the Congress had become slack again. It was nowhere near giving itself the kind of headstart it had aimed for. At the time Rahul held his Phulpur rally, the Party had only declared its candidates for less than half the seats in the state. It had not executed its earlier plan. The BSP and the SP had finished their lists even before the Congress was half way through the exercise.

In another part of UP, in Rahul's constituency and his mother's, concerns over Sonia Gandhi's illness once again raised expectations of Priyanka's participation in electoral politics. Speculation about the younger sibling contesting the next Lok Sabha election from either Amethi or Rae Bareli was back to pre-2004 levels of intensity. At that point, locals, including Congress supporters and assembly-level Congress leaders, had expected Priyanka to contest the Lok Sabha elections in 2004, and had even prepared for it. A few days before Rahul's Phulpur show in November 2011, a local Congress leader in Amethi said, 'With madam [Sonia Gandhi] planning to go abroad for treatment soon, expectations of Priyanka replacing her in the next election have grown. Earlier, her children were young, now they have grown up. She can contest the election and we are preparing the ground for that.'

It was only in early 2004, when Rahul visited Amethi with Priyanka, that the speculation about his entering politics began. On that tour of Amethi, Priyanka had been Rahul's guide. She had taken him around the constituency and introduced him to people there. In March that year, the Congress announced Rahul's candidacy; Sonia Gandhi vacated the Amethi seat for him and moved to Rae Bareli. Priyanka stayed away from contesting elections, but remained an active campaigner, both at the parliamentary and the assembly level elections. Of the ten assembly constituencies in Amethi and Rae Bareli, the

Party won seven in the 2007 elections. Without this, its tally of a mere 22 of 403 would have seemed even more inconsequential. 'The Party's performance in the area was largely due to Priyanka's active campaigning,' said an insider. Besides, she continues to participate actively in the development initiatives run by the Rajiv Gandhi Foundation and the Rajiv Gandhi Mahila Vikas Pariyojana (RGMVP). She closely monitors the self-help groups (SHGs) run by the RGMVP. Towards the end of 2011, the SHGs had almost three lakh women from different parts of the state involved in small-income generation and employment initiatives. Before the 2004 election, the number had stood at a mere 6,000. Running the SHGs had provided Priyanka with a window of access to thousands of families in the constituencies through the women who worked there.

Back in New Delhi, the Congress has denied reports of Sonia's ill health. Details of her trip to the US in August for the treatment of an undisclosed ailment have never been made public. Asked about the Congress president's health and a possible visit in the future to the US for follow-up treatment, Janardhan Dwivedi, the Party's general secretary and chief of the media department, snapped at a reporter on 8 November that the information was 'total rubbish', adding, 'I don't even consider it worth a response.' Dismissing a question about whether Sonia Gandhi would be fit enough to campaign in the UP elections, Dwivedi declared she would be addressing a rally at Chamoli in Uttarakhand the very next day to kick off the Party's election campaign in the hill state. Only, on the day of the rally, he was made to eat his words and announce: 'The Congress president is running a fever. Her visit to Uttarakhand has been cancelled.' Instead, Sonia's address was read out.

Even in Delhi's Congress circles, murmurs of the scam-ridden UPA using Priyanka as a trump card in 2014 have been doing the rounds. So, when Dwivedi was asked whether she would indeed enter the arena of active politics, he said, 'They themselves decide who in the family has to do what and, right now, Rahul is in politics.' In early 2004, when Priyanka had taken her brother around Amethi, the national media—particularly the news channels—had followed them on the tour. On one occasion, an informal interaction turned into an impromptu press conference. Asked if she was going to contest the election or if she would agree to play a bigger role, Priyanka had shot back at a journalist, almost laughing: 'Who will give me a larger role? I have to decide for myself.' Given the casual setting, the editor of an international news service said she had answered 'like a Gandhi'. Unfazed, she had responded, 'I have been hearing this about myself since I was fifteen. And I hear of my entering politics mostly from you [the media].' If the Congress performs poorly in UP, the results will again trigger the pre-2004 'Rahul or Priyanka' debate, irrespective of whether or not she takes the plunge.

Epilogue

Though it doesn't seem as though 10 Janpath and 24 Akbar Road would be adjoining addresses, the two compounds are separated only by a wall that is approximately ten feet high. One of the gates of Sonia Gandhi's heavily guarded residence—the one that visitors, including top notch party officials and ministers, use—opens onto Akbar Road. Every time election results pour in or there is a party-related celebration, the 150-yard stretch between this gate and the entrance to the Congress headquarters becomes one long stage on which performers shout themselves hoarse singing paeans to the first family. Dates like 9 December or 19

June, Sonia's and Rahul's birthdays respectively, are, of course, occasions for celebration. Jagdish Sharma is a small-time Delhi Congressman who appears on such occasions leading a troupe of others like him. They dance and shout slogans, to the tune of hired bands that play at weddings, wishing Sonia or Rahul a long life. If it's Sonia's birthday, the slogans range from 'Mother Sonia' to 'Mother India'; if it is Rahul's, then the slogans revolve around wishing him a long life and demanding that he take over the party, the government and the country forthwith.

As Sonia Gandhi slowly withdraws from public life, her message to sycophantic Congressmen is to not celebrate her birthday. The focus has slowly shifted to Rahul, whose birthday continues to be celebrated outside 10 Janpath whether or not he is in town or even in the country. Amid bursting crackers, Sharma and his bunch of enthusiastic fellow Congressmen get their pictures taken holding Rahul's posters. They even cut a cake and pretend to feed it to the posters. Year after year, TV news cameramen shoot the cacophonic display of sycophancy and transfer the footage from the broadcast vans stationed outside the Congress headquarters. Often these images of the frenzy surrounding the event are telecast in a loop for a few seconds in the occasional bulletin as fillers, as part of the 'Rahul Gandhi birthday' package. Sometimes, this footage comes in handy when the channels show opinion polls that point out how Rahul remains the most favoured PM-in-waiting.

Sharma is one of the many Congressmen who cry themselves hoarse shouting slogans. Congress leaders, irrespective of their position and experience in the party, do not hesitate to declare that Rahul Gandhi has come of age, that he must take over the party and/or the government with no further delay. Manmohan Singh is no different. Year after year, since Rahul Gandhi became party general secretary, Singh has spoken about how he would be only too happy to make way for 'younger people' to take over. In May 2009, as he returned to power as prime minister, Manmohan Singh said, 'It is my wish to have Rahul in the Cabinet but I have to persuade him to be in the government.' A few days later he repeated himself, 'So far [Rahul] has not agreed but I have not given up hope.' Seven months later, he said it again, 'I have tried many times but not succeeded, I will be very happy to have him in the ministry.'

On 19 June 2011, Rahul Gandhi turned forty-one. Senior Congress leaders used the occasion to announce that he had the right qualities, instincts and experience needed to become the prime minister of India. 'I think it is time that Rahul can become the prime minister. He is now [past] forty and he has been working for the party for the last seven to eight years,' Digvijaya Singh said in Bhopal. It was left to a lesser leader, party spokesperson Jayanthi Natarajan, to clarify that the party wasn't going to effect a change immediately. 'Manmohan Singh is the prime minister and will continue in the post,' Natarajan clarified. But she also made it clear, 'Rahul Gandhi is the future leader of the party and the country.' Less than a month after the incident, in July 2011, during his announcement of what he said would be the last Cabinet reshuffle in UPA-II's tenure, Prime Minister Manmohan Singh said for the umpteenth time, 'I requested [Rahul] several times to join the Cabinet but he has said he has responsibilities in the organization.' In that reshuffle, incidentally, Natarajan was made a minister.

After Rajiv's death, Sonia did not formally take charge of the Congress. Initially, she stayed away from politics. She slowly started taking a keen interest in the affairs of the Congress but by the time she became its president in 1998, it was nearly seven years after her husband's assassination. Rajiv, an even more reluctant entrant into politics, was pushed into the thick of things by the deaths of his brother Sanjay and mother Indira. Indira is said to have reluctantly joined Shastri's Cabinet in 1964. In less than two years, she succeeded him as the prime minister. Rahul's reluctance is very much of a piece with his family's attitude.

Rahul has tried to model a large part of his politics around some of Mahatma Gandhi's and Nehru's ideas. There is an interesting exchange between the two that merits mention here. In response to Gandhi's suggestion that Nehru take over as party president in 1929, Nehru wrote to him on 13 July that year as to why he preferred to stay away from the post:

My own personal inclination always is not to be shackled down to any office. I prefer to be free and to have time to act according to my own inclinations. But for years past I have been tied down to various offices and have had to give a great deal of my time to routine and other work to the exclusion of other matters to which I would have liked to attend to. On my return from Europe I had the fixed intention of spending a few months at least in some village areas, more or less cut off from outside activities. I wanted to try to organise them according to my own ideas but even more so I wanted to educate myself and try to get at the back of the mind of the villager . . . So far as I am concerned the presidentship will thus be a burden to me.

Rahul, though in his second term as the Lok Sabha MP from Amethi, has repeatedly turned down 'requests' from the prime minister and has chosen not to work as a minister. Theoretically, it may be possible for any MP from the ruling party not to be a minister despite the prime minister asking him to be so, but legislative duties are not a matter of choice. Rahul has continually chosen to neglect parliamentary proceedings and instead spend time picking up lessons in the field. Several eyebrows were raised when, in his eighth year in Parliament, he told a group of villagers in western UP during his padyatra that he had learnt more from them than he had in Parliament. 'When we sit in Delhi or Lucknow, we don't get to know ground realities. I have not learnt as much in Lok Sabha as I learnt from you,' he said. The statement immediately put the spotlight on Rahul's performance in Parliament and it turned out that he had been a reluctant participant as a lawmaker.

From May 2009 till the monsoon session of 2011, Rahul had not asked a single question of the ministers in the current Lok Sabha, unlike his counterparts. MPs from other political parties had asked, on an average, 119 questions in the two years of the fifteenth Lok Sabha. Data compiled by PRS Legislative Research, a New Delhi-based organization that tracks the performance of legislators, revealed that—against the national average of about sixteen debates that every Lok Sabha MP participated in—Rahul drew a naught. He had performed better as a first-time MP in the UPA I government, but only in comparison to himself. His attendance was 63 per cent compared to the national average of 70 per cent. He had asked three questions in five years during the question hour as opposed to an average of nearly 180 questions each by other MPs. He had also participated in five debates as against the national average of thirty.

During his second term, Rahul asked no questions and had no debates in his account, with the exception of a zero hour mention on 26 August 2011. Beyond that lone intervention, he largely remained a mute spectator to the Lok Sabha proceedings. While attendance of the MPs went up to 77 per cent in the current Lok Sabha, Rahul's average has been a low 47 per cent. Leave aside learning from the Lok Sabha, a student with this kind of attendance would be barred from taking exams for not having been present in enough classes. But in politics, the exams are of a different sort. 'In the Indian system,' said contemporary historian Mahesh Rangarajan, 'unlike the US, you are not judged by your performance in Parliament.' Rangarajan clearly meant that what an MP says in Parliament, or doesn't, needn't fetch him or her votes or popularity. He cited the example of former prime minister Indira Gandhi. 'For the initial ten years that she was in the Rajya Sabha, she made very limited interventions. She hardly spoke,' he said, adding that her silence in Parliament in those years did not stop her from becoming one of the toughest prime ministers India has had.

Those who track Parliament even more closely have a different view. 'It is very important for every MP to engage in the parliamentary process,' said M.R. Madhavan, head of research at PRS Legislative Research. 'The main role of the MP is to represent national interest: your role in making laws, which does not apply just to your constituency.' The number of days Parliament meets annually has been reduced by half since the 1950s. It is about sixty-five sittings every year now. This leaves more time for MPs to work outside Parliament but at the same time, it should leave them with less scope for absenteeism when Parliament is in session.

The standard reply from the party when questioned about Rahul's refusal to take up a ministerial job or to play a more active role in Parliament is that he is focused on his organizational task—of rebuilding the Congress from the grassroots. 'He deliberately keeps a low profile. If he asks a question, ministers will bend over backwards to please him. You can expect Congress MPs to laud everything he says. This kind of situation is best avoided,' a junior minister considered close to Rahul said when asked about his leader's poor performance in the Lok Sabha.

Of the few times that Rahul has spoken in Parliament, he has nearly always stuck to the issues on which he seems to be building his entire politics: Uttar Pradesh, and the India of the poor and the marginalized. In his maiden speech in 2005, he used the opportunity to slam the Uttar Pradesh government, then headed by Mulayam Singh Yadav, while drawing attention to the plight of sugarcane growers:

The Uttar Pradesh Government made a statement in the Supreme Court on 11 January 2005 stating that the private sugarcane mills had paid all the arrears to the cane farmers of Uttar Pradesh. However, the Uttar Pradesh Cane Commissioner later said on the TV news channel Aaj Tak that a sum of Rs 517 crore which were the arrears for the year 2002–03 had not yet been paid. This is extremely unfair to our farmers. I urge upon the Government of India to see that the State Government complies with the directions given by the Supreme Court.

Two years later, while addressing a rally at Muzaffarnagar, UP, Rahul reminded the people present about that speech. 'The sugarcane farmers face problems. Are you happy that I have to raise their problems in Parliament? Isn't it the duty of the state government to look after them?' He had learned early in politics that while it is important to keep one's ear to the ground and pick up the signals, it is equally important to harp on every little step taken to improve the lot of the people.

Every speech Rahul has made in Parliament has almost always been peppered with personal experiences from his travels across the country. The tours he has undertaken to educate himself about the concerns of the *aam aadmi* have him approaching the issues in a personalized manner where, instead of talking numbers, Rahul has brought names and stories of ordinary Indians into the Lok Sabha. During Budget 2006–07, while drawing attention to the education system which he said is 'crushing the aspirations' of thousands of children across India, he cited an example from his visit to a village school a year ago.

I walked up to a village student and asked him, '*Beta, bade hokar kya banoge* [What will you become when you grow up]?' The silent stare which I got in reply disturbed me. In school after school, I have asked this question. And in school after school, I have got no answer. Many students, teachers and parents believe that our system is a dead end.

More such examples followed, one of them of a jobless university topper.

Two years ago I visited a university in a northeastern state. I met a university topper who was unemployed. Now, here is an exceptional person, a person who has followed the path laid out for him perfectly. But after fifteen years of hard work he discovers that our system has led him nowhere. It has crushed his dreams.

On the rare occasions that Rahul has stood up to make a point, senior leaders in the Lok Sabha have listened indulgently as adults would to a child making his first appearance on stage. The times when he fumbled, there were encouraging smiles from the benches. When he spoke during the debate on the trust vote in July 2008 after the Left pulled out on the Indo-US nuclear deal, he started out by saying, 'I decided that it is important at this point not to speak as a member of a political party, but to speak as an Indian.' This time around Opposition leaders immediately jumped up to protest. 'All are Indians,' said one member of the House. 'Please speak in Hindi,' demanded another MP, BJP's Karuna Shukla who is also former prime minister Atal Bihari Vajpayee's niece. This was not how Rahul's earlier speeches had been received. Most MPs had patiently given him the time and the space to make his point. A surprised Rahul gathered his wits and addressed Shukla in Hindi, 'Madam,' he said, 'I will speak in Hindi and English both. All I am saying is that you are our elder, please listen to us. You don't have to agree with us but just listen to us.' To the others he said,

I completely agree with you that you are also an Indian and you should also speak as an Indian. I would go further to say that you do speak as an Indian and I do not doubt that. So, I decided that what I would do is that I would take a step that a lot of our politicians normally do not do. I decided that I will make a central assumption in my speech. The assumption is that everybody in this House, regardless of which party they come from, whether they come from the BJP or the Shiv Sena or the Samajwadi Party or the BSP or the Congress Party, speaks in the interest of the nation.

Amid interruptions, he told the stories of two women from Vidarbha in Maharashtra—a region infamous for suicides by debt-ridden farmers—and how nuclear energy would change the fate of their families. 'Three days ago, I went to Vidarbha and there, I met a young lady who has three sons. The young lady, Sasikala, a landless labourer, lives with Rs 60 a day,' he said, and spoke about how her sons dream of a bright future but are forced to study with the help of a little brass lamp because the house has no electricity. When he started to speak about Kalawati, who had nine children, some MPs interrupted and a few of them laughed. 'I am glad you find that funny,' Rahul said to them, 'But Kalawati is a person whose husband committed suicide. So, I would urge you to respect her.' As more protests and interruptions followed, Speaker Somnath Chatterjee said, 'I think the Parliament of India is reaching its lowest position—nadir!' The House was adjourned and when it met after the lunch recess, Rahul picked up from where he had left.

After initial disturbances, he was allowed to speak uninterrupted. Only now, instead of Kalawati, he spoke of the woman from Vidarbha as 'Mrs Kala' evoking laughter from the benches. Rahul, too, stopped to smile sheepishly. A familiar mood of indulgence settled on the benches as Rahul went on to finish his speech. While

concluding, he candidly spoke of the lesson he had learnt
that day.

> We might have different views about how this country
> should be built. We might have different opinions on
> what we should do. But essentially we sit in this room
> together and we have to solve our problems together.
> This is what differentiates us and this is what gives us
> our true power—that any voice can be heard in this
> room, that any voice can disrupt any other voice in
> this room. I am being serious. It is uncomfortable for
> me. But I am very proud of it that every voice can be
> heard in this country.

Despite all the attention that followed Rahul's mention
of Kalawati's struggles, she never got compensated for her
husband's suicide. The land he tilled was not in his name
and his death was never registered as a farmer's suicide.
In 2010, her son-in-law killed himself and the following
year, her daughter.

In the initial years, Rahul openly admitted in
Parliament, 'I am new to politics and still have a lot to
learn.' The simple issues that he raised as a first-time MP
might have sounded naive to seasoned parliamentarians
but those were pertinent points coming from a political

novice. MPs are indeed supposed to keep an ear close to the ground and bring issues of concern to Parliament, where laws are enacted. In the second term, it is only natural to expect an MP to graduate towards making more assertive and pertinent interventions in policymaking. But that hasn't happened in Rahul's case. In seven years, he has participated only in five debates.

This is perhaps one reason that he sometimes finds himself ill-equipped to tackle questions that are unexpectedly asked of him. During his 2011 padyatra in Uttar Pradesh, when Rahul was faced with tough questions from the peasants he met, he simply ignored those questions. At Bajna village, he chose not to reply to a farmer who said inflation was hurting them as much as land issues. This was the second time in two days that he had ignored the question. At Chandpur, a young man questioned him on corruption and Rahul said ministers were sent to jail and action was taken. He took no supplementary questions from the young man and asked him to read the papers for details.

Rahul's stance on many issues of pressing national importance is either not known or is seen as simplistic. His utterances, inside and outside Parliament, have not provided observers with enough material to see him as a fully rounded personality—as a politician and citizen.

Jim Yardley of the *New York Times* wrote in June 2010, one year after the UPA's resounding comeback in the Lok Sabha polls:

> Despite his aura of inevitability, Rahul largely remains an enigma. India is an emerging power, facing myriad domestic and international issues, but he remains deliberately aloof from daily politics. His thoughts on many major issues—as well as the temperature of the fire in his stomach—remain mostly unknown.

Like most other journalists who tried and failed to get an interview, Yardley did not succeed in gaining access to Rahul. If India is the world's largest democracy, the US claims to be the greatest, and Yardley's observations—as a foreign correspondent who grew up in the US and is writing about the next leader of the Indian National Congress and possibly even India—are both interesting and telling:

> Rahul is using his enormous popularity to broaden the party's political base, steering clear of more contentious policymaking. That could help position the Congress party to win an outright national majority—though it does little to illuminate what

he would do with a mandate if he won it . . . Rahul is omnipresent in the media, and his face is plastered on untold numbers of billboards and political posters. His public image is as a humble, serious man, if somewhat shy, even as his name invariably tops polls ranking the country's 'hottest' or 'most eligible' bachelors. Yet he rarely grants interviews, including for this article, and only occasionally conducts news conferences. Reporters are often tipped to his appearances at one village or another, but often all they get is a photograph—which inevitably appears in newspapers around India.

His daily life is cloaked in secrecy, which makes it an irresistible if elusive topic for the Indian media. One news station ran a lengthy report after obtaining a 10-second video clip of Rahul riding his bicycle in New Delhi.

Yardley's article quoted Pratap Bhanu Mehta, once a member-convener of the National Knowledge Commission, a high-powered advisory body to the prime minister of India, and now the president of the New Delhi-based think tank, Centre for Policy Research. 'What most people still have a hard time figuring out is, "What is Rahul Gandhi's vision?"' Mehta told the *New York*

Times. Mehta had met Rahul privately and spoke highly of him, yet his concerns—with regard to what exactly the Congress leader's ideas are—remained unresolved. 'It is still not apparent to a lot of people what his own deep political convictions are.' In another interview, to rediff.com's Sheela Bhatt, as UPA-II neared its second year in the saddle in the beginning of 2011, Mehta appeared to have been able to diagnose the problem more clearly.

We know Rahul Gandhi is extremely important for the party. He is mobilizing the new constituency for the party. Somehow, he seems to be operating on the assumption that there is a difference in political mobilization and government and governance. I think Rahul Gandhi is making the biggest mistake in thinking that political mobilization and outreach can happen independently of your record in government. That somehow you can be a big national leader without taking a clear public stand on the major issues of the country.

Speaking to one of the authors some months later, Mehta said he had nothing more to add to his analysis. Nothing had changed. 'A leader is judged by his actions. People will judge [Rahul] the same way too.'

If one goes by opinion polls that appear in the media from time to time, Rahul remains the most popular contender for the prime minister's position. Yet, his projected charisma does not quite seem to turn the Congress's fortunes in places where the party does not have a strong base any longer. An opinion poll by NDTV in 2009 found that 46 per cent of the respondents believed that Rahul would make a better prime minister than Manmohan Singh, who lagged behind by 8 per cent. Though a majority (55 per cent) felt that Rahul would be the next prime minister, a greater percentage of voters also felt that there would be no change of guard at the prime minister's level before the 2014 elections. The same year, a C fore survey conducted for the newsweekly *Open* soon after the Congress's surprise revival in Uttar Pradesh found that a majority of the respondents (46 per cent) felt that Rahul should have become the prime minister in 2009 instead of Manmohan Singh. Opinions clearly had changed since 2005 when a survey conducted for *India Today* had found that a majority of Indians (63 per cent) felt that dynastic politics was unacceptable.

The truth of electoral politics in India is, however, often at variance with the findings of such surveys and polls. In the 2004 elections more than 240 political families contested and nearly two dozen political dynasts were elected as members of Parliament. The *Open* magazine survey of 2009 also revealed that nearly 60 per cent of the people felt that Rahul was more accessible than other politicians. A majority went to the extent of describing him as incorruptible and as a young, energetic leader with a clean image. A whopping 64 per cent was of the opinion that Rahul should contest the 2012 assembly election in Uttar Pradesh as the Congress candidate for chief minister—an option which senior Congress leaders had ruled out saying that Rahul was a national leader with a national image and could not be confined to one state. Besides, despite the inroads which the Congress has made in Uttar Pradesh, surveys have indicated that though Mayawati might have lost some ground, the battle is far from over. The Congress, surveys showed, isn't yet in a position to wrest control from the Bahujan Samaj Party. A CVoter opinion poll on Uttar Pradesh, conducted for the *Sunday Indian*, showed that while 64 per cent felt that BSP will suffer if Rahul goes all out with his poll campaign, a majority still wanted to see Mayawati as the chief minister of the country's most populous state. Mayawati, it was felt, had already consolidated her votes among minorities; infrastructure development under her had improved and her schemes to uplift the Dalit population would fetch her votes.

Assembly electoral results since 2009 have shown that Rahul's magic does not work in state elections. The party paradropped him into every election campaign, and he attracted listeners but not voters. Though the Congress did not fare as badly in the 2011 assembly elections as it had in Bihar, it did not do too well either. Rahul's nominees discovered the hard way that it takes more than just blessings from the high command to win elections against strong opponents. In Kerala, for instance, despite the anti-incumbency vote against the Left front government, the Congress-led United Democratic Front barely scraped through. Of Rahul's eighteen nominees, only eight won. He had selected twenty-four Youth Congress candidates for the elections in Tamil Nadu, West Bengal and Assam—seven each in the eastern states and ten in Tamil Nadu. Not a single candidate won in Tamil Nadu, where the Congress and its senior alliance partner, the DMK, took a severe beating at the hands of the Jayalalithaa-led challenge to the incumbent government. In West Bengal, where the Congress played a junior partner to Mamata Banerjee's Trinamool Congress, riding an anti-Left wave, four of Rahul's seven nominees won. Assam was the only state where all seven nominees returned from the polls as members of the legislature. Here the Congress government returned to power in the absence of a serious challenger. Clearly, in these states, local factors rather than the pull of youth led the voters to decide on which way they went.

Electoral politics is as much about winning as it is about making your opponents lose. Rahul Gandhi's next big challenge is the UP assembly polls of 2012. Before he (or his party on his behalf) can stake a claim to the post of prime minister in 2014, the UP elections must show that his party-building exercise is fetching results. Those around him, however, hasten to clarify that Rahul is in no hurry to be the prime minister. According to a member of his core team,

He is looking at the position that the party will occupy in one to two decades' time from now. The Congress will have new members, those who have come through a process of election via the Youth Congress. It will have strong presence in every part of the country and the current old guard of the party would have phased out by then.

Before he stakes a claim to the position of the prime minister, Rahul will also have to tackle the contradictions between his left of centre stance and the government's reformist approach. He has often spoken of the contrast between the 'two Indias', of the rich getting richer at the cost of the poor, and has taken pro-poor positions. He has been able to influence similar decisions by the government. But special packages for weavers or farmers and guaranteeing rural employment or food security are not the only decisions the UPA government has taken. Commenting on these conflicting positions, Sitaram Yechury, CPM politburo member and MP, said, 'I don't want to personalize this but if anybody else wants to pick up our issues and our ideas, they are very welcome. I only wish that they don't just look at this as a descriptive term but also try to understand why this is happening. The reforms which it is following on the one hand and its *aam aadmi* concerns on the other are the fundamental contradictions of UPA-II.'

***

August 2011 was an eventful month for the UPA government. It threw up new challenges that would require swift action and not merely ideas. The monsoon session of Parliament began with the government appearing increasingly confused under growing pressure from an agitation led by the Maharashtra-based activist Anna

Hazare and his support group. Called Team Anna, the group included bureaucrat-turned-activist Arvind Kejriwal, Kiran Bedi, a retired (and India's first) woman Indian Police Service officer, civil rights lawyer Prashant Bhushan and his father, former law minister Shanti Bhushan. The group was supported by a host of other people, including a number of film stars. They had been demanding the institution of a strong anti-corruption body—the Lokpal—that successive governments had managed to put off for more than four decades. After the first round of protests in April 2011, in which Hazare and his supporters insisted that the government's version of the Lokpal Bill was toothless and that their version be adopted by Parliament instead, the government formed a joint drafting committee including Hazare and his supporters on one side and some of the government's key ministers on the other. The committee failed to reach a consensus as the government insisted on keeping the prime minister, the judiciary and the lower bureaucracy out of the purview of the proposed anti-corruption watchdog. As the talks fell through, Hazare threatened to go on an indefinite fast at New Delhi from 16 August to press for his team's version of the Lokpal Bill, which they called the Jan (People's) Lokpal Bill.

The government was already on the back foot when the Parliament session began on 1 August. Yet, at this crucial juncture, Sonia Gandhi was missing, as was Rahul. Congress leader Janardhan Dwivedi announced on 4 August that Sonia was ill and undergoing surgery abroad, which would keep her in hospital and away from party affairs for three weeks or so. Her family was with her, which was why she and Rahul had not been able to attend Parliament. It was also announced that the Congress president had appointed a four-member committee—consisting of her political secretary Ahmed Patel, Janardhan Dwivedi, Defence Minister A.K. Antony and Rahul Gandhi—to look after party affairs in her absence.

Just like in the beginning of 2011, murmurs of Rahul being made the working president of the Congress began. 'Now, again, after the Congress president's surgery, Rahul is being asked to take on a larger role,' said a young Congress MP considered close to him. 'This time, he is not as reluctant, as you can see. The coming few months are going to be interesting.' Ever since the UPA-II began floundering under the weight of scams and its own inaction, there have been murmurs of Rahul replacing Prime Minister Manmohan Singh. Sonia's illness gave rise to rumours that he would replace her soon as the party's president rather than be appointed working president. Reluctant as ever to take up a party position, Rahul, however, did slowly start looking at party matters beyond just the affairs of the IYC and the NSUI.

As a precursor to the eventual takeover, the Congress decided that he would unfurl the national flag at the Independence Day function at the party headquarters in New Delhi on 15 August 2011. The party office is a busy place on normal days but, during Sonia's visits, it is sanitized and more security is deployed. The police and the SPG swung into action and made similar security arrangements for Rahul. He attended the function and saluted the national flag wearing a Nehru cap, but made sure it wasn't him but party treasurer Motilal Vora who hoisted the flag. The function was followed by a meeting of the Congress top brass, called at Rahul's behest, to discuss the impending crisis that Hazare's fast would trigger. During the meeting Rahul is said to have insisted that the party spokesperson and the government's crisis managers had made a mistake by attacking the activist in their media briefings. On the previous day, Congress spokesperson Manish Tiwari had completely misjudged the public sentiment when he alleged that Hazare was not above corruption. Tiwari, faced with a possible law suit from Hazare and having earned Rahul's displeasure, publicly expressed regret for his statement.

On 16 August, as Hazare prepared to launch his fast against the government, the Delhi Police arrested him on the pretext that it apprehended a breach of peace. With Parliament in session and the government already in disarray, all hell broke loose. Both houses were stalled and there was outrage over the arrest. Fuelled by non-stop television news coverage, the number of Anna's supporters slowly grew. Even those who found fault with his team's stubborn insistence on its version of the bill opposed the government's action of arresting Anna. Home Minister P. Chidamabaram tried to hide behind the plea that the police had acted on their own, apprehending a breach of law and order. But his defence found little acceptance.

By that evening, the Delhi Police requested the court which had sent Hazare to judicial custody in Tihar jail to release him. A triumphant Hazare, however, refused to leave the jail premises till the government agreed to let him proceed with his fast. The government relented and Hazare led a victory procession two days later to the Ramlila Maidan in central Delhi and continued his fast. As criticism of the government increased, Prime Minister Manmohan Singh made an appeal to Hazare, in Parliament, to stop the fast, with the assurance that the government would come up with a strong Lokpal. Hazare and his team relented, but only a little. He insisted on an assurance from Parliament and a resolution that his key demands—including new ones—would be met.

On Friday 26 August 2011, Rahul broke his silence in Parliament. During the zero hour that day, just a few minutes after noon, he made an unscheduled intervention to speak on the Lokpal issue and the swelling protests that had brought the government to its knees. This was the first time since he returned in May 2009 as the Amethi MP to the 15th Lok Sabha that he spoke in Parliament. As mentioned earlier, he was known more for his silence and absence than his interventions in Parliament. For about fifteen minutes, amid protests and interruptions from the Opposition, he spoke on the Lokpal impasse. The BJP protested Speaker Meira Kumar's special allowance to the Congress leader. As Opposition leader Sushma Swaraj later explained, Rahul spoke without notice and for fifteen minutes instead of the permitted three minutes for an unscheduled intervention. It turned out to be a rather busy day in Parliament. A couple of hours after he spoke, nearly a dozen young Congress MPs staged a protest outside, in an attempt to counter the attack on Rahul by the BJP inside Parliament.

On the face of it, Rahul Gandhi's zero hour mention in Parliament was at best a few months late or a few hours early—he is an important leader of the Congress and with the Bill having been under consideration for so long, he could have spoken earlier. The tussle with Anna Hazare, who had the backing of a large segment of civil society, had begun months earlier. Even Hazare's second fast was ten days old by the time Rahul Gandhi spoke. Parliament was all set to debate the fresh demands Hazare had laid out in a few hours; Rahul could have spoken then. Yet, he chose his own time. He wanted to be heard separately and, in a way, set the agenda for the Party. What he said was not in consonance with what Prime Minister Manmohan Singh had said a day earlier—appealing to Anna Hazare to end the fast. Rahul, instead, said that more important than ending the impasse was tackling the issue of corruption.

I believe that the real question before us, as representatives of the people of India today, is whether we are prepared to take the battle against corruption head on. It is not a matter of how the present impasse will resolve, it is a much greater battle. There are no simple solutions. To eradicate corruption demands a far deeper engagement and sustained commitment from each one of us. Witnessing the events of the last few days, it would appear that the enactment of a single Bill will usher in a corruption-free society.

I have serious doubts about this belief. An effective Lokpal law is only one element in the legal framework to combat corruption. The Lokpal institution alone cannot be a substitute for a comprehensive anti-corruption code. A set of effective laws is required. Laws that address the following critical issues are necessary to stand alongside the Lokpal initiative: Government funding of elections and political parties; transparency in public procurement; proper regulation of sectors that fuel corruption like land and mining; grievance redress mechanisms in public service; delivery of old age pension and ration cards; and continued tax reforms to end tax evasion.

'Madam Speaker,' he announced, in the course of his mention, 'Why not elevate the debate? Let us take it further and fortify the Lokpal Bill by making it a constitutional body like the Election Commission of India. I feel the time has come for us to seriously consider this idea.'

Rahul then attacked the protestors and their methods, almost putting an end to the rapprochement process.

A process divorced from the machinery of an elected Government that seeks to undo the checks

251

and balances created to protect the supremacy of Parliament, of this House, sets a dangerous precedent for our democracy. Today, the proposed law is against corruption. Tomorrow, the target may be something less universally heralded. It may attack the plurality of our society and our democracy. India's biggest achievement is our democratic system. It is the life force of our nation. I believe we need more democracy within our political parties. I believe in government funding of our political parties. I believe in empowering our youth, in opening the doors of our closed political system, in bringing fresh blood into politics and into this House. I believe in moving our democracy deeper and deeper into our villages and our cities.

Anna Hazare's Jan Lokpal agitation seemed to be finding resonance with the youth of India. And young voters moving away could affect the fortunes of the Congress, particularly those of Rahul. A young Congress MP admitted:

Our worry has been that it is the Congress party that has brought important Acts like the rural guarantee scheme, the right to information and compulsory education. Yet, even the youth seem more interested in joining the anti-government protests. We need to go back and tell them what the Congress stands for.

That the protests did not have a specific caste or communal base was a source of greater worry for Rahul. He had been speaking in favour of moving beyond these criteria and had been exhorting voters to choose parties that deliver good governance. Anna Hazare's movement threatened to take away that agenda and use it against the UPA for delivering poor governance. The first indication that Hazare's interventions in governance would be multi-pronged came two days later, when he triumphantly broke his fast. He announced that his fast was merely being suspended and the agitation had other goals to achieve. Caught in scam after scam, time was running out for the Congress and the UPA. If the urban middle class, especially the youth, moved away, Rahul's efforts of years would be negated.

The Party was quick to take its cue from Rahul's intervention in Parliament. Party spokesperson Abhishek Manu Singhvi said, 'I want to make it clear that the Congress party has always stood for a comprehensive and strong Lokpal. Indeed it has made its stand clear through its general secretary that it would like the Lokpal to be even stronger, even more elevated in the sense of a constitutional status body.' Note that Singhvi was not just an ordinary MP, but also chairman of the Standing Committee on Justice looking into the Lokpal Bill.

The BJP, on its part, was quick to run down Rahul's views. 'I always believe that when you have no solution to offer to a problem you talk of systemic changes and get into generalizations,' said Arun Jaitley, leader of the Opposition in the Rajya Sabha. His counterpart in the Lok Sabha, Sushma Swaraj, while speaking on the Lokpal debate on 27 August, sarcastically remarked that Rahul's intervention was actually 'an address to the nation'. The BJP was feeling triumphant over the pro-Jan Lokpal protests turning into an anti-UPA sentiment. It hoped to gain from it. In the words of Bhagalpur MP and BJP spokesperson Syed Shahnawaz Hussain, 'A lot of BJP workers and voters were part of the protests. Though they did not carry the BJP flag, they were our supporters. Inside Parliament, we are the custodians of the fight against corruption. Raja and Kalmadi are in jail because of us.'

On the day Hazare broke his fast, 28 August 2011, party president Gadkari released a statement from Nagpur, addressing Hazare:

We promise you that the BJP will always be ready
to rally around you and march forward under your
leadership, should the need arise any time in future
to fulfil your dream of a truly democratic corruption-
free India. Anna, rest assured, we will not let you
down in and outside Parliament. Nor will we allow
the government to betray you any further.

Gadkari's offer to let Anna lead and have the BJP
follow obviously ruffled a lot of feathers within the
party leadership. The party leaders were worried that
their party president Nitin Gadkari was too eager to
cede the space of the Opposition to the likes of Anna
Hazare and yoga guru Ramdev. However, the Congress's
worry, particularly Rahul's, was much bigger. On the one
hand the BJP seemed to be gaining from the movement
and, on the other, Hazare seemed to be slowly weaning
the youth away from Rahul. The Congress general
secretary had tried to adopt the Gandhian model of
politics in more ways than one. He had chosen to stay
outside the government and encouraged padyatras,
himself participating in one. In fact, before he took up
his padyatra in western UP, egged on by his open support
for the idea, various Youth Congress leaders, including

MPs, had undertaken padyatras across the country. The IYC website also lists a code of conduct for padyatras. And Rahul had once even led a silent sit-in in front of Mahatma Gandhi's statue in Parliament during the first term of the UPA.

At a closed-door Youth Congress brainstorming session for senior functionaries in Thiruvananthapuram, Rahul had asked the participants to emulate the Gandhian methods of people's movements. 'Don't get involved in everything, Rahulji told us giving the example of Mahatma Gandhi. Focus on a few key issues but make sure those issues are important for the people, just like Mahatma Gandhi did, he said,' recalled an IYC official who had attended the session.

Rahul had fully backed Sonia Gandhi's renunciation of the prime minister's position in 2004, on the call of her 'inner voice', and her resignation in 2006—acts which were popularly perceived as Gandhian. But, of late, the symbol of peaceful resistance, the Mahatma, had been appropriated by those protesting against the Indian National Congress and its current set of leaders. Hazare's fast, that lasted for days—with him ensconced in front of a huge picture of the Mahatma—made a strong anti-government statement drawing protestors to the streets. Ironically, the Congress was threatened by a man who wanted to use the Gandhian satyagraha against it. Perceived to be a Gandhian and even a modern-day Gandhi, because of some smart spin-doctors in his team, Hazare could be seen as doing exactly that.

While Rahul followed a passive approach in his politics promising to usher in slow change, Hazare was more aggressive. He dictated a deadline to the government for putting anti-corruption measures in place. Anna Hazare and his team could well be the catalysts of the change Rahul desired. And it appears that Rahul can no longer control the pace of that change. The anti-government sentiment, in effect anti-Congress sentiment, and the exigencies thrown up by Sonia's illness will decide the speed at which Rahul's plans for the future are implemented.

Select Bibliography

Adams, Jad and Whitehead, Phillip. 1997. *The Dynasty: The Nehru-Gandhi Story*. London: Penguin and BBC Books.

Akbar, M.J. 2002. *Nehru: The Making of India*. New Delhi: Lotus Roli.

Alexander, P.C. 2004. *Through the Corridors of Power: An Insider's Story*. New Delhi: HarperCollins.

Assam Pradesh Youth Congress. 2009. *Aam Aadmi ka Sipahi: A Viewbook*. Shillong.

Bayly, Susan. 1999. *Caste, Society and Politics of India: From the Eighteenth Century to the Modern Age*. Cambridge: Cambridge University Press.

Bose, Ajoy. 2008. *Behenji: A Political Biography of Mayawati*. New Delhi: Penguin Viking.

Brass, Paul R. 1990 (reprint 2004). *The Politics of India since Independence.* Cambridge: Cambridge University Press.

Chandra, Bipan, Mukherjee, Mridula and Mukherjee, Aditya. 1999. *India after Independence: 1947–2000.* New Delhi: Penguin.

Chatterjee, Partha. Ed. 1997. *State and Politics in India.* New Delhi: Oxford University Press.

Dev, Arjun. Ed. 2011. *Gandhi–Nehru Correspondence: A Selection.* New Delhi: National Book Trust.

Frank, Katherine. 2001. *Indira: The Life of Indira Nehru Gandhi.* London: HarperCollins.

French, Patrick. 2011. *India: An Intimate Biography of 1.2 Billion People.* New Delhi: Allen Lane.

Gandhi, Indira. 1986. *Letters to a Friend 1950–1984. Correspondence with Dorothy Norman.* London: Weidenfeld & Nicolson.

Gandhi, Sonia. 1992. *Rajiv.* New Delhi: Penguin.

Guha, Ramachandra. 2007. *India after Gandhi.* London: Picador.

Hansen, Thomas Blom and Jaffrelot, Christophe. Ed. 1998. *The BJP and the Compulsions of Politics in India.* New Delhi: Oxford University Press.

Hasan, Zoya. Ed. 2002. *Parties and Party Politics in India.* New Delhi: Oxford University Press.

Hutheesing, Krishna Nehru. 1969. *Dear to Behold: An Intimate Portrait of Indira Gandhi.* Mumbai: IBH Publishing Company.

Kaviraj, Sudipta. Ed. 1997. *Politics in India.* New Delhi: Oxford University Press.

Kidwai, Rasheed. 2003. *Sonia: A Biography*. New Delhi: Penguin Viking.

Kothari, Rajni. 1970. *Politics in India*. New Delhi: Orient BlackSwan.

Masani, Zareer. 1975. *Indira Gandhi: A Biography*. London: Hamish Hamilton.

Malhotra, Inder. 2006. *Indira Gandhi*. New Delhi: National Book Trust.

Mitta, Manoj and Phoolka, H.S. 2007. *When a Tree Shook Delhi: The 1984 Carnage and Its Aftermath*. New Delhi: Roli Books.

Mukherjee, Pranab. Ed. 2011. *Congress and the Making of the Indian Nation*. Vol. 1 & 2. New Delhi: Academic Foundation.

Nayar, Kuldip. 1971. *India: The Critical Years*. Delhi: Vikas Publications.

Kumar, Ravinder and Sharma, Hari Dev. Ed. 1998. *Selected Works of Motilal Nehru*. New Delhi: Vikas Publishing House.

Pai, Sudha. 2002. *Dalit Assertion and the Unfinished Democratic Revolution: The Bahujan Samaj Party in Uttar Pradesh*. New Delhi: Sage Publications.

Raman, B. 2007. *The Kaoboys of R&AW: Down Memory Lane*. New Delhi: Lancer Publishers.

Singh, Khushwant. 1999. *A History of the Sikhs: 1839–2004*. Vol. 2. New Delhi: Oxford University Press.

Singh, Patwant and Malik, Harji. 1985. *Punjab: The Fatal Miscalculation*. New Delhi: Patwant Singh.

Thakur, Sankarshan. 2006. *Subaltern Saheb: Bihar and the Making of Laloo Yadav.* New Delhi: Picador.

Newspapers, Periodicals, Websites and Television Shows

Miscellaneous

Bal, Hartosh Singh. 2005. New Team Must Have Rahul Gandhi as General Secretary of the AICC. *Tehelka.* 11 June.

Crime and Politics in UP. 2006. *Times of India.* 2 December.

Dhume, Sadanand. 2010. India's Gandhi God-Kings. *Wall Street Journal.* 20 July.

Dutt, Barkha. 2009. In Conversation with Priyanka Gandhi. NDTV 24x7. 24 April.

Gandhi Dynasty Poised for Power. 2004. CNN.com. 14 May.

Gandhi, Sonia. 2010. Letter to the Congresspersons. *Congress Sandesh.* August.

Garewal, Simi. 1991. *India's Rajiv.*

George, Varghese K. 2009. All New Hands on the Deck. *Hindustan Times.* 15 February.

Gupta, Shekhar. 2008. Walk the Talk with Rajnath Singh. NDTV 24x7. 16 November.

Indian National Congress. 2009. *CWC Resolution.* 17 May.

Lohade, Unisha. 2011. Rahul Gandhi Goes Dutch at New Yorker. *Hindustan Times.* 3 April.

Majumdar, Diptosh. 2011. Rahul Gandhi Hand in Disclosure Move. *Times of India*. 24 October.

NDTV & GfK-MODE Opinion Poll. April 2009.

Rahul Thanks Sikhs for Giving India 'a forward-looking Prime Minister'. 2011. *The Hindu*. 30 July.

Ramachandran, Rajesh. 2003. Priyanka's Amethi Visit Renews Debate on Her Joining Politics. *Times of India*. 21 April.

Schneider, Bill. 2004. Gandhi Has Power, but Declines Post. CNN.com. 21 May.

Singh, Akhilesh Kumar. 2004. Brahmins Pin Hope on Rahul, Priyanka. *Times of India*. 1 May.

Singh, Kanishka. 2005. Dreaming of India in 2010. *Seminar*. December.

Smith, William E. 1984. Indira Gandhi: Death in the Garden. *Time Magazine*. 12 November.

Srivastava, Piyush. 2010. Rahul Plans Chariot Ride on Maya Turf. *Mail Today*. 20 March.

Swami, Praveen and Ramakrishnan, Venkitesh. 1997. The Politics of Blackmail. *Frontline* (29 November–12 December).

TSI CVoter Opinion Poll on Uttar Pradesh. 2011. *Sunday Indian*. 2–8 May.

Vivek, T.R. 2004. Want to be CEO of Rahul Gandhi's firm? *Business Standard*. 24 June.

Yadav, Puneet Nicholas. 2008. Rahul Gandhi's Dig Irks St. Stephen's. *DNA*. 23 October.

Yardley, Jim. 2010. India's Young and Poor Rally to Another Gandhi. *New York Times*. 4 June.

Open

Bal, Hartosh Singh and Jha, Dhirendra K. 2009. Up in the Air. 25 April.

Jha, Dhirendra K. 2010. The Congress and Its Fear of Elections. 6 November.

From INC to Congress Inc. 9 January 2010.

The Great Congress Reconquest. 31 October 2009.

The Rahul Effect: 110%. Open C fore survey. 16 October 2009.

The Indian Express

Bhat, Virendra Nath. 2009. Why Mayawati Loves to Hate Former Aide P.L. Punia. 25 May.

Chatterjee, Manini. 2006. Gandhi vs Gandhi. 9 October.

Ghose, Sagarika. 2004. I'm Young, I Have Ideas, I Believe I Can Bring Change. 30 March.

Gopinath, Vrinda. 2004. My Girlfriend Is Spanish: Rahul Gandhi. 28 April.

Masood, Bashaarat. 2011. In Valley, Rahul Waits for Questions—and Gets Some Answers Too. 27 September.

PM Can't Just Say I Am a Good Man but Every Other Man Is Making Money. 26 December 2010.

Select Bibliography

Singh, D.K. 2007. Rahul Meet Focuses on Poll Challenges. 27 September.

———. 2008. Rahul's New Team in Place. 18 January.

———. 2008. Marksheets in Hand, MPs, MLAs Line Up for Rahul's Talent Search. 12 June.

———. 2008. Congress Plans Grassroots Revival, to Fall Back on Gandhi. 5 September.

———. 2008. Rahul: If I'd Not Come from Gandhi Family, I Wouldn't Be Here. 21 October.

———. 2009. Why the Congress Is Going Solo. 29 March.

———. 2009. Why Rahul Is Known as 'Priyanka's Brother' Here. 24 April.

———. 2009. Rahul Talent Hunt Set to Go National. 11 July.

———. 2009. Mission 2012: Congress Begins Search for UP Candidates. 11 August.

———. 2010. Dear Rahul . . . Yours Sincerely Manmohan Singh. 11 April.

———. 2010. Sonia Raps Hooda Over Caste Violence. 30 April.

———. 2010. The First Thousand Days. 15 June.

———. 2010. Rahul Gets His First Reality Check 4/234. 25 November.

———. 2010. Rahul's 'New Youth Cong': Same Old Same Old. 14 December.

TV Journalists Quizzed for 'Stealing' NSUI Papers. 25 January 2009.

Outlook

276 Feels Good, Bar the Grey Areas. 26 April 2004.

Bhaumik, Saba Naqvi. 2008. Borne Supremacy. 6–12 May.

———. 2004. Fear of the Family. 26 April.

Bhushan, Ranjit. 2002. Salaam Sonia. 13 May.

Congress's Hot Potato: Rahul Gandhi Kicks Up a Storm in UP. 30 April 2007.

Ghimire, Yubaraj and Rattanani, Lekha. 1995. It's Head Hunting Time. 13 December.

Gupta, Smita. 2009. A Question of the Heir & Now. 1 June.

Jha, Prem Shankar. 2003. Who Is an Indian? 3 November.

Kang, Bhavdeep. 2003. Origins, Destinations. 3 November.

———. 2004. Silver Linings, Clouds. 10 May.

———. 2004. The Angelic Hierarchy: *Outlook* MDRA Opinion Poll. 16 February.

———. 2004. Tortoise Troops in. 24 May.

King is Singh. *Outlook Election Extra*. May 2009.

Mehra, Sunil. 1998. The Man Nobody Knows. 16 February.

Mukerjee, Sutapa and Kang, Bhavdeep. 2003. On Popular Demand. 4 August.

Naqvi, Saba. 2010. Seventh-year Hitch. 13 December.

———. 2010. The Lady in the Saree. 22 March.

Pratap, Anita. 2004. Swinging Blue Genes. 19 April.

Reddy, Sheela. 2009. A Nose for Politics. 11 May.

Singh, Kanishka. 2004. Why Sonia Is Like John Kerry. 12 April.

Ups and Downs. 4 March 2002.

India Today

Aiyar, Shankkar. 2006. Smart Move. 3 April.

Prasannarajan, S. 2005. Sonia Gandhi: India's Phoenix. 17 January.

Sahgal, Priya. 2007. Family First. 30 April.

——. 2009. The Rahul Offensive. 19 May.

The New Mrs G. 2 December 2002.

From the Internet

1984 Sikh Carnage Was Wrong: Rahul. http://www.indianexpress.com/news/1984-sikh-carnage-was-wrong-rahul/387614/

Gandhi, Rahul. Plight of Sugarcane Growers in Uttar Pradesh and Other Parts of the Country. http://164.100.47.132/LssNew/psearch/Result14.aspx?dbsl=1778

Gandhi, Rahul. *Budget Speech, 2006–07.* http://164.100.47.132/LssNew/psearch/Result14.aspx?dbsl=5113

Gandhi, Rahul. Further Discussion on the Motion of Confidence in the Council of Minister Moved by Dr. Manmohan Singh on the 21st July, 2008. http://164.100.47.132/LssNew/psearch/Result14.aspx?dbsl=10243

Gandhi, Rahul. Need of a Comprehensive Political Programme to Eradicate Corruption. http://164.100.47.132/LssNew/psearch/Result15.aspx?dbsl=5349

Gandhi, Rahul. 2004 affidavit. http://eci.nic.in/GE2004_
Affidavits/Uttar%20Pradesh/Affidavits/21/RahulGandhi/
RahulGandhi_SC1.html

Gandhi, Sonia. 18 May 2004. Speech. http://in.rediff.com/
election/2004/may/18sonia2.htm

Stung by Verdict, Maya Turns to Dalits Again. http://election.
rediff.com/report/2009/may/19/loksabhapoll-stung-by-
verdict-mayawati-turns-to-dalits-again.htm